Folk Art Landscapes
for every season

JUDY DIEPHOUSE & LYNNE DEPTULA

NORTH LIGHT BOOKS
CINCINNATI, OHIO
WWW.ARTISTSNETWORK.COM

Dedication

Our dedication is quite simply made to the people who inspire and encourage us to be the best we can be. This includes our wonderful families, from parents down to grandchildren, and all of the creative and generous students and shop owners we have had the pleasure to work with. Not a seminar goes by that we don't learn at least one new technique or receive inspiration from teaching. And when we get home—yes, we do spend time at home—our families make us feel grounded and loved. Thank you to all the wonderful people in our lives!

Acknowledgments

We would like to acknowledge the terrific team at North Light Books... KATHY KIPP, CHRISTINE POLOMSKY and BETHE FERGUSON for their professional and enthusiastic abilities. They make creating, painting and writing these books a joy! Thank you!

We would also like to thank the suppliers of our surfaces, brushes and paints for their generosity. When we design a book, we very often walk around trade shows and "pick" surfaces from various vendors. We think it is wonderful to create for these pieces. The quality brushes and paints that are available for all decorative painters makes painting these designs effortless.

Other fine North Light Books are available from your local bookstore, art supply store or direct from the publisher.

05 04 03 02 01   5 4 3 2 1

Library of Congress Cataloging-in-Publication Data

Diephouse, Judy, 1943-
    Folk art landscapes for every season / Judy Diephouse & Lynne Deptula.--
    1st ed.
        p.   cm.
    Includes index.
    ISBN 1-58180-117-3 (pbk. : alk. paper)
        1. Painting. 2. Folk art. I. Deptula, Lynne, 1954- II. Title.

TT385 .D545 2001
745.7'23—dc21   00-066422 CIP

Editor: Bethe Ferguson
Production Coordinator: Kristen Heller
Designer: Wendy Dunning
Photographers: Christine Polomsky and Al Parrish

METRIC CONVERSION CHART

to convert	to	multiply by
Inches	Centimeters	2.54
Centimeters	Inches	0.4
Feet	Centimeters	30.5
Centimeters	Feet	0.03
Yards	Meters	0.9
Meters	Yards	1.1
Sq. Inches	Sq. Centimeters	6.45
Sq. Centimeters	Sq. Inches	0.16
Sq. Feet	Sq. Meters	0.09
Sq. Meters	Sq. Feet	10.8
Sq. Yards	Sq. Meters	0.8
Sq. Meters	Sq. Yards	1.2
Pounds	Kilograms	0.45
Kilograms	Pounds	2.2
Ounces	Grams	28.4
Grams	Ounces	0.04

About the Authors

JUDY DIEPHOUSE and LYNNE DEPTULA both live in Grand Rapids, Michigan, with their families. They met at a West Michigan Decorative Painters Paint-In where Judy was teaching and Lynne was just beginning to discover the joys of decorative painting. Several years later, they began a partnership that focuses on painting for large art shows… really, it was paint and make an income, or get a "real" job! As the years passed, they evolved from painting for art shows to teaching for conventions, designing pattern packets, writing decorative painting books and travel teaching. Quite a glorious journey! Now they have published thirteen books and over one hundred pattern packets with more ideas to come. Please contact them at the addresses below or through their Web site: http://www.distinctivebrushstrokes.com.

JUDY DIEPHOUSE
1674 Hall St. SE
Grand Rapids, MI 49506
Phone: (616) 241-2937
Fax: (616) 241-4766
E-Mail: DistinctJ@aol.com

LYNNE DEPTULA
7245 Cascade Woods Dr. SE
Grand Rapids, MI 49546
Phone: (616) 940-1899
Fax: (616) 940-6002
E-Mail: Dbrush1@aol.com

Table of Contents

one

Getting Started

PAINTS

We used Delta Ceramcoat and DecoArt Americana acrylic paints to paint the projects in this book. These are non-toxic, water-based acrylic paints sold in 2-ounce (59ml) bottles. Shake the bottles well before using to make sure the binder is mixed with the pigments.

These paints can be thinned with water to an ink-like consistency for linework and strokework. We use water to thin the paints, but these two paint companies offer several products you can mix with the paints for blending, strokework and slowing the drying time. You may wish to experiment with them.

BRUSHES

All of the brushes used in this book are from Scharff Brushes, Inc., P. O. Box 746, Fayetteville, Georgia 30214, 1 (888) SCHARFF.

The series used are:
 #142 —flats
 #458 —liners
 #406 —rounds
 #482 —scrollers or script liners
 #550 —wash
 #670 —mop
 #429 —filberts
 #750 —deerfoot

Acrylic brushes are generally made from synthetic fibers, such as Golden Taklon, because they hold up better when used with acrylic paints. The condition of your brushes plays a major role in the quality of your painting.

It is difficult for anyone to achieve nice strokework, linework or good floats with brushes that have swelled or have loose hairs sticking out of them. Several good brands are on the market, but like other things, you get what you pay for. To clean the brushes, we recommend DecoArt Americana's Brush Cleaner.

ADDITIONAL SUPPLIES

Water Basin

Several brands of water basins are available, but a good one will have ridges across one section of the bottom for you to pull your brush across. This will loosen and clean the paint from your brush. There should be grooved holders on the other side to hold brushes in the water and prevent the paint from drying in the brush. A high divider helps keep the dirty water separate from the clean water.

Stylus

A good stylus is helpful for applying the pattern to the project, making fine dots and adding details on your painting. It often comes with a fine point end and a heavier point end.

Palette Knife

A palette knife is used for mixing two or more colors together.

T-Square and Clear Flexible Ruler

A T-square or ruler helps you apply the lines of your pattern straight. They are available at most office supply and art stores.

Sponge

A small, round sponge is used to apply clouds and foliage on some of the projects.

Pencils

Always have a supply of sharpened no. 2 pencils and chalk pencils in your paint supplies. If you omit any tracing lines, it

is often easier to freehand the missing line or detail.

Transparent Tape

We recommend using a quality transparent tape. Apply the tape where needed, and seal the edge of the tape with your fingernail to prevent paint from bleeding underneath the tape.

Palette

We use disposable waxed palettes. We do not use a wet palette, since we often request you to blend colors together as a double load or side-load float. It is difficult to achieve a nice blend or float on a wet palette.

Tracing Paper

Tracing paper comes in pads of sheets in a variety of sizes. It is available at art

and office supply stores. After you trace the design on the tracing paper, place the paper on the prepared project and tape down one side. Slide a piece of graphite paper under the tracing, and retrace the design with the stylus. We use white and gray graphites—white on dark backgrounds and gray on light backgrounds. If your graphite is brand-new, you may want to wipe it with a paper towel to remove the excess graphite. After your painting is complete and dry, erase any visible tracing lines with a soft eraser before you varnish the project.

Foam Brush or Roller

A foam brush or small foam paint roller is useful for basecoating or staining the project piece. Both are available from hardware, craft and paint stores.

two

Basic Painting Techniques

Side-Load Float

Use a flat brush in good condition, dampened slightly with clean water. Touch one corner of the brush into paint and work in one spot on your palette. Firmly brush back and forth to spread the paint gradually across the brush. The brush should have strong color on one side of the brush and gradually lighten to clean water on the other side of the brush. After the brush is properly loaded, use a light touch to stroke in the float.

Double Load

To double load a brush, dip one corner of a slightly dampened brush into color no. 1, covering about half of the brush. Next dip the opposite corner of the brush into color no. 2. Stroke the brush back and forth on your palette until you have a soft blend of color from one side of the brush to the other. Flip the brush over and blend the other side for even coverage.

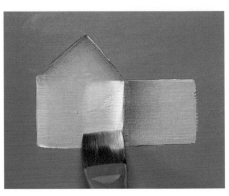

Highlight Floats

Load the brush properly for a side-load float in the requested highlight color. With the highlight color side of the brush next to the area to be highlighted, apply some pressure and softly pull the brush through the highlight area.

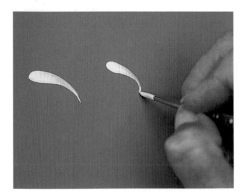

Comma Stroke

Load the brush generously with paint. Apply pressure to the head of the stroke. Release the pressure, raise to the tip of the brush and paint the tail of the stroke.

Shading Floats

Load the brush properly for a side-load float in the requested shade color. With the shade color side of the brush next to the desired area, apply some pressure and softly pull the brush through the shade area.

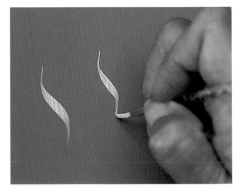

S-Stroke

Load the brush generously with paint. Start the stroke on the tip of the brush, pulling slightly to the left. Apply pressure to the brush while pulling slightly to the right. Release the pressure, returning to the tip of the brush and again pulling slightly to the left.

One-Stroke Leaf

Start the leaf standing on the chisel edge of the brush. Apply pressure to make the fullest part of the leaf. Slowly lift the brush, allowing the bristles to return to the chisel edge. This stroke is identical to the comma stroke except it does not have the long tail. Double load the brush to achieve a double-loaded one-stroke leaf.

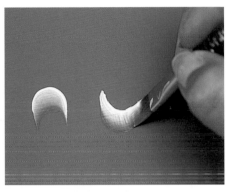

Double-Loaded C-Stroke

Double load your flat brush with one color on one side of the brush and another color on the other side. Blend on your palette. Starting on the chisel edge of the brush, apply pressure to draw the letter **C**, releasing the pressure to return to the chisel edge and complete the letter.

Flip-Flop Float

Load the brush as in a side load float, with the concentration of color on one side of the brush. Apply the color side of the brush along the center of the area to be highlighted, then flip your brush over, applying color on the other side of the highlighted area. Make sure to overlap your color areas and soften into each other.

HINT ❯ *Often painters butt the color floats next to each other and thus get a ridge of paint in the center of the highlight area. Make sure to overlap the color sides of the floats.*

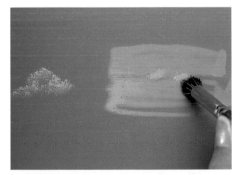

Dry Stippling vs. Wet Stippling

Using an old brush or a deerfoot brush, dip the tips of the brush into paint. Tap the brush on your palette or a paper towel to blend and remove excess paint. Stipple with an up-and-down motion using a light touch. Dry stippling is done on a dry surface. For wet stippling, first slightly wet the area with clean water, then softly stipple on the color. The wet background will allow the paint to soften out and slightly bleed into the background.

Linework

Thin your paint with water to an ink-like consistency. Load the brush fully with paint. Using your small finger or the side of your hand to steady yourself, stay on the tip of the liner brush and pull the linework toward you. The lighter the touch, the thinner the line; the heavier the touch, the thicker the line.

HINT ❯ *Look just beyond the tip of the liner brush to where you want the line to go, rather than at the tip of the brush. The hand will follow the eye and help you paint a straighter line.*

11

Herb Planter

I have seen the plans for this garden shed in magazines for years. I would love to have a similar one in my backyard, but for now I have it on my little herb planter. This planter fits on any window sill and can hold a few culinary herbs for the winter.

paint colors

(D) = Delta Ceramcoat Acrylics; (DA) = DecoArt Americana

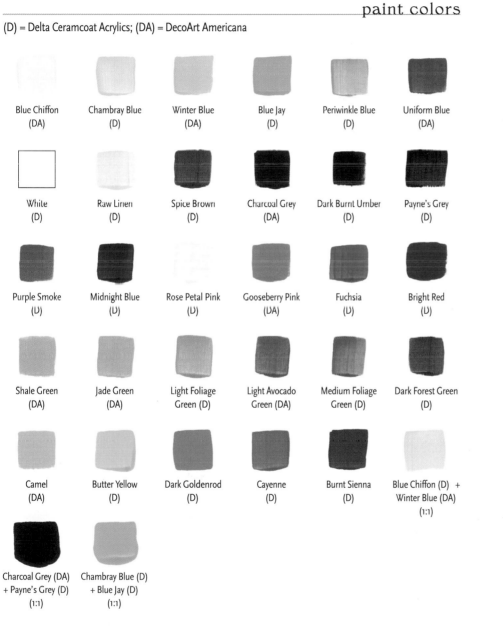

Blue Chiffon (DA)	Chambray Blue (D)	Winter Blue (DA)	Blue Jay (D)	Periwinkle Blue (D)	Uniform Blue (DA)
White (D)	Raw Linen (D)	Spice Brown (D)	Charcoal Grey (DA)	Dark Burnt Umber (D)	Payne's Grey (D)
Purple Smoke (D)	Midnight Blue (D)	Rose Petal Pink (D)	Gooseberry Pink (DA)	Fuchsia (D)	Bright Red (D)
Shale Green (DA)	Jade Green (DA)	Light Foliage Green (D)	Light Avocado Green (DA)	Medium Foliage Green (D)	Dark Forest Green (D)
Camel (DA)	Butter Yellow (D)	Dark Goldenrod (D)	Cayenne (D)	Burnt Sienna (D)	Blue Chiffon (D) + Winter Blue (DA) (1:1)
Charcoal Grey (DA) + Payne's Grey (D) (1:1)	Chambray Blue (D) + Blue Jay (D) (1:1)				

materials

SURFACE
- Wood planter box from Wayne's Woodenware, Neenah, Wisconsin.

BRUSHES
- nos. 2, 4, 8, 14 and 16 flats
- ³⁄₄-inch (19mm) flat
- no. 0 liner
- nos. 4 and 8 deerfoot stipple brushes

ADDITIONAL SUPPLIES
- Minwax Ipswich Pine Wood Finish
- plastic liner for inside planter
- three 2 ¹⁄₂ inch (6.4cm) terra cotta pots
- satin acrylic varnish
- gray graphite paper
- stylus

BASECOAT THE SKY *and* BEGIN THE FOLIAGE

Patterns for Herb Planter

These patterns may be hand-traced or photocopied for personal use only. Enlarge the above pattern at 115% to return to full size. Pattern shown at right is full size.

1 Stain the entire box with Minwax Ipswich Pine Wood Finish. Basecoat the Masonite insert in a mix of Blue Chiffon + Winter Blue (1:1). Trace on the pattern with a stylus and gray graphite paper.

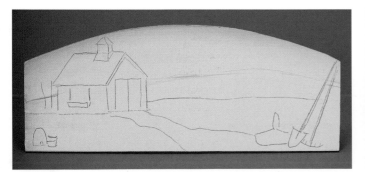

2 Wash the top edge of the sky with a side-load float of Uniform Blue. Wash along the horizon line with a side-load float of Blue Chiffon, and tint with touches of Gooseberry Pink using a ¾-inch (19mm) flat.

3 Using a no. 16 flat, basecoat the back hill with Jade Green, shade the bottoms of the hills with Light Avocado Green and highlight the top with Shale Green. Stipple the trees on the top of this hill in the same colors as the hill using a no. 4 deerfoot. Add touches of Blue Chiffon to the top of the trees to help them fade into the sky.

THE GRASS AREA, FENCE *and* SHED

4 Paint the grass area with a brush mix of Light Avocado Green and Jade Green using a no. 16 flat. With a no. 0 liner, use Dark Burnt Umber and touches of Raw Linen for the tree trunks. With a very light touch, add foliage on the trees, first with Dark Forest Green, then lightly highlight with Medium Foliage Green, Light Foliage Green and touches of White using a no. 4 deerfoot.

5 Create the fence with strokes of Raw Linen and two fine lines for the rails using a no. 0 liner. Shade the fence post with a light touch of Charcoal Grey pulled up from the bottom with a no. 0 liner. Highlight the tops of the fence posts with a touch of White pulled down from the top with the no. 0 liner. Basecoat the path with a brush mix of Raw Linen and a touch of Charcoal Grey using a no. 8 flat. Using a no. 2 flat, touch the dirty brush into Raw Linen, then lightly into Charcoal Grey and/or Payne's Grey. Dab on the stones in the path. When the stones are dry, shade next to the shed door and along the sides of the path with a side-load float of a mix of Charcoal Grey + Payne's Grey (1:1).

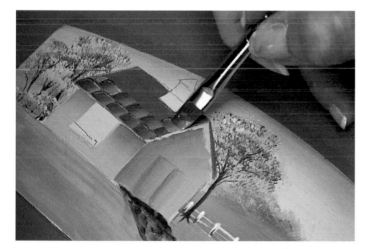

6 Basecoat the shed with a mix of Chambray Blue + Blue Jay (1:1) using a no. 14 flat. Shade with a side-load float of a brush mix of Charcoal Grey and Payne's Grey. Keep the shading soft. Basecoat the roof in Cayenne. Using a no. 8 flat, load the brush in Cayenne. Dip one corner into Spice Brown and the other corner into Dark Goldenrod. Blend slightly on your palette. Stroke on the shingles of your roof.

7 Once the roof is dry, shade from the upper left corner down with a side-load float of a brush mix of Spice Brown and Dark Burnt Umber. Highlight from the lower right corner up with a float of Dark Goldenrod using a no. 16 flat. Basecoat the cupola in White and shade with a brush mix of Charcoal Grey and White. Add some detail lines using the shade mixture with a no. 0 liner. Using a no. 4 flat, base the roof in Cayenne, shade with Spice Brown and highlight with Dark Goldenrod. Paint the windows with a wash of Midnight Blue, and shade on the left side with a side-load float of Midnight Blue. Outline the windows, door and under the roof with White using a no. 0 liner. Base the window box in White.

THE SHED, FLOWERS *and* CLAY POTS

8 Shade the door frame and window box with a brush mix of Charcoal Grey and White using a no. 0 liner. Make the hinges on the door with small lines of Payne's Grey.

9 Using a no. 8 deerfoot and no. 4 deerfoot when needed, stipple in the foliage of the garden starting with light touches of Dark Forest Green. Highlight in any order with Medium Foliage Green, Light Foliage Green, Jade Green and White. Add some branches of the bush with fine lines of Dark Burnt Umber using a no. 0 liner. Shade lightly under the flower beds—by the side of the shed—with a side-load float of Dark Forest Green with a touch of Charcoal Grey added. Also, remember to add some foliage in the window box.

10 Paint the petals of the black-eyed Susans with strokes of Butter Yellow with a Burnt Sienna center using a no. 0 liner. Create delphiniums with touches of a brush mix of Periwinkle Blue and White. Make hollyhocks with touches of a brush mix of Rose Petal Pink and Gooseberry Pink. Add small strokes of Dark Forest Green to indicate leaves. Paint the carpet roses with touches of Rose Petal Pink brush mixed into Fuchsia. Create the blossoms on the butterfly bush with dots of Purple Smoke and White. Make the liatrus with dots of Fuchsia highlighted with a little Rose Petal Pink. Paint the daisies with strokes of White with Butter Yellow centers. Paint the coneflowers with strokes of Fuchsia touched into Rose Petal Pink. Create the centers with cone shapes of Spice Brown. Add dots of flowers in the remaining spaces using any of the above colors.

11 Basecoat the clay pots by the shed door and by the bee skep with Cayenne using a no. 2 flat. Shade one side with Burnt Sienna, and highlight the other side with a brush mix of Cayenne and Rose Petal Pink. Once the pots are dry, stipple in some foliage using the greens of the garden. Using the no. 0 liner, make clumps of dots of Bright Red to indicate geraniums in the pots and window box. Brighten some of the dots with touches of Fuchsia. Add trailing dots of White for hanging flowers. In the clay pot by the bee skep, add stems and leaves with Dark Forest Green and dots of White for blossoms. Paint the rose trellis by the side of the shed with fine lines of White. Create the vining on the trellis with fine lines of Spice Brown. Very lightly stipple the foliage on the vines with Medium Foliage Green. Add some dots of a brush mix of Fuchsia and Rose Petal Pink to denote roses.

THE BEE SKEP, BASKET *and* TOOLS

12 Basecoat the bee skep and basket in Camel using a no. 4 flat. Shade the left side of the bee skep with Burnt Sienna, and highlight the right side with a brush mix of Camel and Butter Yellow. Using a no. 0 liner, add in section lines with Burnt Sienna. Create the hole in the skep with Dark Burnt Umber. Paint the weaves of the basket with a double-loaded no. 4 flat in Camel and Burnt Sienna.

13 Base the metal part of the spade with a brush mix of Payne's Grey and White using a no. 4 flat. Shade with a little Payne's Grey and highlight with White. Paint the metal part of the rake in the same color, only darker. Use Spice Brown shaded with Dark Burnt Umber for both wood handles. Shade the basket next to the tools with Burnt Sienna with a touch of Dark Burnt Umber added. Shade the left side of the bee skep with this mix also. Pull some stems and leaves from the basket with any green on your palette, and add any of the flowers from your garden.

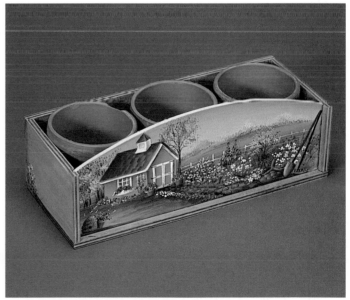

14 Pull some grasses from the lower back corners of the planter using Dark Forest Green with touches of Medium Foliage Green. Add some leaves along these grasses with Medium Foliage Green and any other greens from your palette using a no. 1 liner. With the no. 4 deerfoot, lightly stipple some soil at the base of the grass with Dark Forest Green with a touch of Charcoal Grey added. You may add any of the flowers growing in the garden to these stems and grasses, such as daisies, coneflowers and black-eyed Susans.

15 Allow the painting to dry completely, and erase any visible tracing lines. Varnish at least three coats inside and out with satin acrylic varnish. Line the bottom of the planter with a plastic liner before putting plants in to catch the overflow water. Add your favorite herbs and enjoy.

Harvest Clock

Autumn is my favorite season! The colors are vibrant and inspiring. Judy and I have a lot of fun when traveling during this season calling out paint colors to match the glorious autumn colors we see. Try it—we hope it will inspire you, too!

paint colors

(D) = Delta Ceramcoat Acrylics; (DA) = DecoArt Americana

White (D)	Bridgeport Grey (D)	Driftwood (DA)	Charcoal (D)	Black (D)	Opaque Yellow (D)
Golden Straw (DA)	Antique Gold (DA)	Milk Chocolate (DA)	Burnt Sienna (D)	Dark Burnt Umber (D)	Lima Green (D)
Light Timberline Green (D)	Dried Basil Green (DA)	Medium Foliage Green (D)	Dark Forest Green (D)	Cadmium Orange (DA)	True Red (DA)
Opaque Red (D)	Tomato Red (D)	Black Plum (DA)	Chambray Blue (D)	Prussian Blue (D)	Burnt Umber Oil Paint
Black Green (D)					

materials

SURFACE

- Wooden clock from Wayne's Woodenware, Neenah, Wisconsin. The quartz battery-operated clock works with a 1/4-inch (6mm) shaft and is available from your local craft supply store.

BRUSHES

- nos. 4, 8, 10 and 16 flats
- 1-inch (25mm) flat
- 6/0 and no. 1 liners
- nos. 4, 8 and 10 deerfoot stipple brushes
- 1-inch (25mm) mop brush

ADDITIONAL SUPPLIES

- transparent tape
- Minwax Ipswich Pine Wood Finish
- Winsor & Newton Burnt Umber Oil Paint
- odorless mineral spirits
- soft, clean cloths
- stylus
- small, round sponge
- J.W. Right Step Clear Varnish, satin
- gray graphite paper
- compass or ruler
- black Micron Pigma pen

Pattern for Harvest Clock

This pattern may be hand-traced or photo-copied for personal use only. Enlarge at 143% to return to full size.

BASECOAT, ADD THE SKY *and* SHADE THE HOUSE *and* HILLS

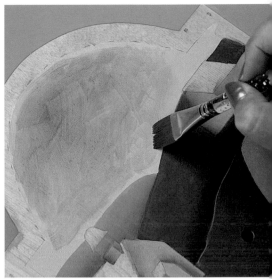

1 Stain the clock with the Ipswich Pine Wood Finish. Let dry completely. Using a stylus and gray graphite paper, transfer the design onto the surface. To keep your edges straight, press strips of transparent tape ⅝ inches (1.6cm) from the outside edge of the clock. You will not be able to tape off the curve. Use a compass or ruler to apply a pencil line ⅝ inches (1.6cm) from the outside edge of the clock and carefully basecoat.

2 Using a no. 16 flat, basecoat the sky area with Chambray Blue. Basecoat the back left hill with Light Timberline Green and the main hills with Dark Forest Green. Basecoat the "crop" hills with Antique Gold on the left and Dried Basil Green on the right. Base the grain in the silo in Antique Gold. Basecoat the small house on the back right side of the clock and the stone foundation on the barn with Bridgeport Grey. Basecoat the schoolhouse with Driftwood and the barn with Tomato Red.

3 Slightly dampen the surface with clean water. Using a no. 16 flat, slip-slap over the sky area with a small amount of Prussian Blue. Concentrate the darkest area of the sky in the top curve of the clock.

HINT ❥ *The slip-slap technique is a loose brush movement similar to the up-and-down motion used to paint a wall.*

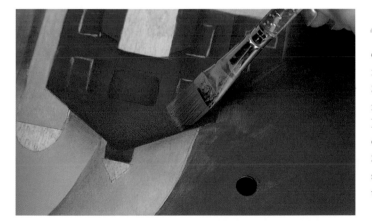

4 Using a no. 16 flat, shade the hills and houses as follows. Shade the lower edge of the back hill with a side-load float of Dark Forest Green. Shade to separate the main hill sections with a side-load float of a brush mix of Dark Forest Green plus a touch of Black. Shade the Antique Gold crop hill with a side-load float of Burnt Sienna. Shade the Dried Basil Green crop hill with a side-load float of Dark Forest Green. Shade to separate the sections of the small house on the back right side of the clock with a side-load float of Charcoal. Shade to separate the schoolhouse sections with a side-load float of sheer Dark Burnt Umber. Shade to separate the sections and define the window areas on the barn with a side-load float of Black Plum.

THE HILLS, WINDOWS, FOLIAGE *and* PATHS

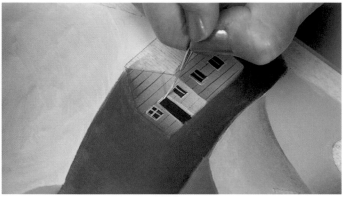

6 Use a no. 4 or no. 8 flat to basecoat all windows and doors with Black. Outline the windows and door on the small house with thin lines of Driftwood. Outline all other windows and doors with thin lines of White.

5 Highlight the main hill with a side-load float of Light Timberline Green using a no. 16 flat. Paint thin horizontal siding lines with Charcoal using a 6/0 liner on the small house. On the barn, paint thin vertical lines of Black Plum to indicate siding lines. Using a no. 16 flat, highlight the small house with a side-load float of a mix of Bridgeport plus a touch of White. Highlight the schoolhouse sections with a mix of Driftwood plus a touch of White. Highlight the barn sections with a side-load float of True Red.

7 Slightly dampen a small, round sponge and touch it into White. Sponge the curved cloud areas onto a slightly dampened surface. Again, working on a slightly dampened surface, softly sponge the background foliage at the horizon line with Black Green.

8 Using a no. 10 flat side-loaded into Driftwood, horizontally streak the paint to create the curved path areas. Notice how the paths are wider at the front edge and become increasingly narrow as they approach the doors of the buildings.

THE PATHS, CROPS *and* SILO

9 Side load Dark Burnt Umber on a no. 16 flat, and loosely shade the outside edges of the paths.

10 Using a no. 4 deerfoot, lightly stipple curved rows of crops in the fields with Dark Forest Green. Add dots of Cadmium Orange with your stylus to indicate pumpkins in the Antique Gold field.

11 Paint short, choppy lines using a 6/0 liner and Golden Straw to indicate straw throughout the silo and in the open door of the barn.

12 Using a no. 4 flat, basecoat the silo cap with Charcoal. Using a no. 8 flat, highlight the top curve of the silo cap with a side-load float of Charcoal touched into White. Paint thin wire lines of Charcoal on the silo using a 6/0 liner. Highlight several of the wires in the middle of the silo with hit-and-miss short lines of White.

HINT ❧ *This hit-and-miss technique allows you to add random spots of highlight to several areas.*

THE STONEWORK *and* TREES

13 Loosely double load a no. 4 flat with Charcoal on one side and Driftwood + White on the other side. Smudge in small random-shaped ovals to indicate individual stones.

14 Using a 6/0 liner and Charcoal, loosely outline each stone.

15 Using a no. 16 flat, reinforce the first shaded areas and shade the stonework to match the barn sections with a soft side-load float of Dark Burnt Umber. Highlight the left edges of the stonework sections with a soft side-load float of White.

16 Using a no. 1 liner and Dark Burnt Umber, pull thick tree trunks into thin branches as indicated on the pattern.

THE HOUSE DETAILS, FOLIAGE *and* FENCE

17 Using a no. 1 liner double loaded into Charcoal and White, paint short horizontal lines to indicate steps in front of the doors. Paint the porch railing on the small house with thin linework of Black. Using a stylus, dot the doorknob with White.

18 Using a no. 4 and/or no. 8 deerfoot, softly stipple in the following foliage areas. In front of the small house and in front of the barn, stipple bushes with a brush loaded into Dark Forest Green and tipped into Lima Green. Keep the Lima Green edge of the brush to the top of the bushes. In front of the schoolhouse, stipple bushes with a brush loaded into Dark Forest Green and tipped into Opaque Yellow. Keep the Opaque Yellow edge of the brush to the top of the bushes. In the lower left corner of the clock, anchor the design by stippling bushes with a brush double loaded into Dark Forest Green and Medium Foliage Green.

19 Slightly dampen the surface with clean water. Use a no. 8 and/or no. 10 deerfoot to paint the various trees. Stipple the green trees with Medium Foliage Green, the yellow trees with Opaque Yellow and stipple the red trees with Opaque Red.

20 Using a 6/0 liner and Bridgeport Grey, paint the fence posts and fence railings onto the design. Highlight the left side of the fence posts, and hit-and-miss on the fence railings with short lines of White.

DETAIL THE SCHOOL, CHICKENS *and* APPLE TRIM

22 Use a no. 1 liner to paint indications of the chickens and rooster. Basecoat the chicken bodies with White and the heads with Burnt Sienna. Basecoat the rooster body with Milk Chocolate and add linework of True Red for the head and tail. Paint all feet and beaks with small lines of Black.

21 Using a no. 4 flat, basecoat the school bell with Opaque Yellow. Shade the left side of the school bell with a side-load float of Burnt Sienna. Using a no. 8 flat, no. 10 flat, or no. 1 liner brush, basecoat the roof areas with Black. Underline the roofs with linework in White. Using a no. 4 flat, basecoat the school sign with a wash of White. Outline the sign with Black. Using a black Micron Pigma pen, letter the sign. Add the weather vane with a 6/0 liner using Black.

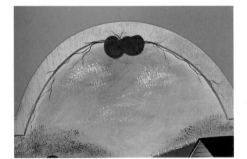

23 Remove the transparent tape. Using a no. 1 liner and Dark Forest Green, paint a border line around the entire design area. Using a no. 10 flat, basecoat the apples with Tomato Red. Using a 6/0 liner and slightly thinned Dark Burnt Umber, pull thin, loose areas of vining from either side of the apples.

24 Using a no. 10 flat double loaded and overblended into Dark Forest Green and Driftwood, paint one-stroke leaves sparingly along the vining. Shade to separate the apples with a side-load float of Black Plum.

25 Using a no. 10 flat, highlight the apple on the left and the smile area on the full apple with a side-load float of a mix of Cadmium Orange plus a touch of Opaque Yellow. Using a no. 4 flat corner-loaded heavily into White, paint small **C**-shaped petals to form the apple blossom petals.

THE APPLE TRIM *and* ANTIQUING

26 Using a no. 4 flat loosely double loaded into Burnt Sienna and Golden Straw, "smudge" oval-shaped flower centers into the middle of the apple blossom flowers. Paint small one-stroke leaves sparingly along the vining using a no. 4 flat and slightly thinned Dark Forest Green plus a touch of Black. Using a 6/0 liner and Dark Burnt Umber, paint short lines for the apple stems. Paint a small highlight stroke of Golden Straw in the middle of the highlight area of the full apple.

27 Using a 1-inch (25mm) flat corner-loaded into a small amount of Dark Forest Green plus a touch of Black, softly shade the lower corners of the clock. This helps soften the design into the surface.

28 Using a 1-inch (25mm) mop brush, apply one layer of J.W. Right Step Clear Varnish. Let cure twenty-four hours. Using a soft cloth and a small amount of odorless mineral spirits, dampen the edges of the schoolhouse clock. The mineral spirits will make the oil paint easier to blend once it is applied to the surface. Rub a generous amount of Burnt Umber oil paint onto the edges of the clock, softening the paint back into the surface with a circular motion and a dry, soft cloth. Let dry completely. Complete the varnishing by brushing on two to three additional layers of J.W. Right Step Clear Varnish.

29 Attach the clockwork following the instructions on the package of the clock face. Add a battery and enjoy!

Country Cottage Mailbox *and* Stamp Box

Keep your desk area clutter-free with this darling tin mailbox and matching stamp box. Perfect for the beginner painter… learn some fun new techniques and be finished in no time!

paint colors

(D) = Delta Ceramcoat Acrylics; (DA) = DecoArt Americana

White (D)	Raw Linen (D)	Bridgeport Grey (D)	Charcoal (D)	Wild Rose (D)	Deep Burgundy (DA)
Pale Yellow (D)	Sea Grass (D)	Dark Forest Green (D)	Black Green (D)	Tide Pool Blue (D)	Wisteria (DA)
Purple Smoke (D)	Khaki Tan (DA)	Burnt Umber (D)	Dark Burnt Umber (D)	Khaki Tan (DA) + Black Green (D) (1:1)	

materials

SURFACE

- Metal mailbox is available from your local builder's supply store. The small wooden stamp box is available from Viking Woodcrafts.

BRUSHES

- nos. 4, 8, 10 and 16 flats
- ¾-inch (19mm) flat
- 6/0 and no. 1 liner
- nos. 8 and 10 deerfoot stipple brushes

ADDITIONAL SUPPLIES

- Rustoleum Light Gray Auto Primer
- J.W. Right Step Clear Varnish, satin
- stylus
- gray graphite paper

Pattern for Stamp Box

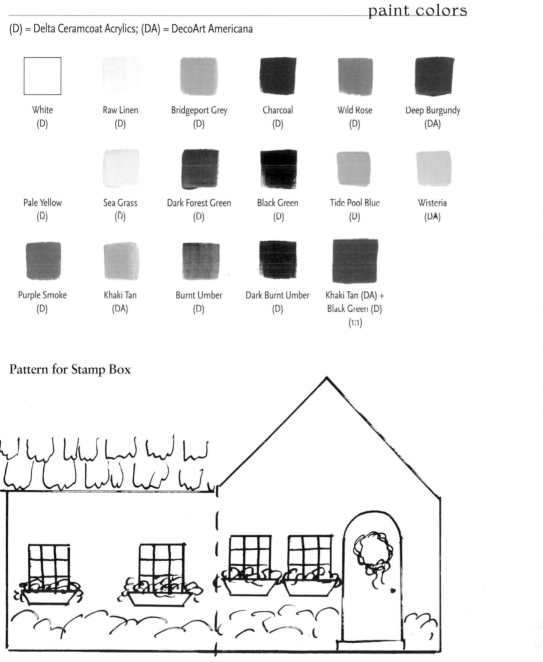

This pattern may be hand-traced or photocopied for personal use only. Pattern shown here is at full size.

Pattern for Country Cottage Mailbox

This pattern may be hand-traced or photocopied for personal use only. To return the pattern to full size you must first enlarge the pattern 200%, then enlarge that pattern 135%.

THE BRICKS *and* WINDOWS

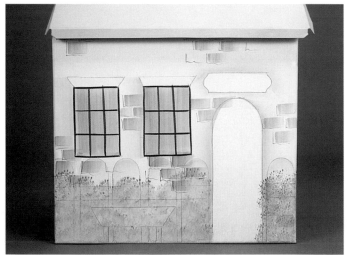

1 Basecoat the mailbox with Rustoleum Light Gray Auto Primer. Let cure several days to allow the paint to adhere to the tin. Basecoat the stamp box with Raw Linen. Using a stylus and gray graphite paper, lightly transfer the pattern onto the mailbox and stamp box. Use a ¾-inch (19mm) flat and a very light, loose load of Charcoal, Khaki Tan and White to paint patches of bricks randomly over the surface of the mailbox. Repeat this step on the stamp box, except use a no. 10 flat to paint the bricks. Use a 6/0 liner and a thinned brush mix of Khaki Tan plus a touch of Charcoal to loosely outline the left and lower edges of the bricks. Add looseness to the design by painting several areas of just outlining next to the bricks.

2 Using a ¾-inch (19mm) flat and very sheer Charcoal, basecoat all windows. Use a 6/0 liner and slightly thinned Charcoal to outline the windows and paint the window pane lines. Let dry. Dampen the surface with clean water. Using a no. 10 deerfoot, lightly stipple in the background foliage with a mix of Black Green + Khaki Tan (1:1). Let the moisture on the surface soften and diffuse the paint into the surface. Using a ¾-inch (19mm) flat side loaded into a mix of Khaki Tan plus a touch of Charcoal, softly float behind the doors, windows and signs.

THE FENCE, SHINGLES *and* HOUSE DETAILS

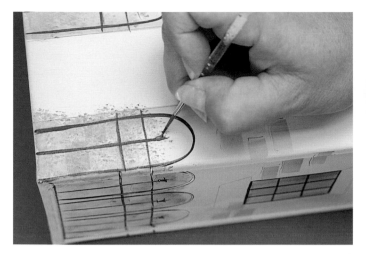

3 Using a no. 1 liner and Charcoal, paint the linework and small one-strokes that compose the metal fence. Highlight the tips of the metal spikes, and hit-and-miss where one metal railing crosses another with short lines of Charcoal mixed with a touch of White.

4 Use a ¾-inch (19mm) flat to basecoat the roof with Khaki Tan. While the roof is still wet, tip the dirty brush into a loose mix of Bridgeport Grey and/or White, and stroke from the bottom edge of the roof up in individual strokes to form the shingles. Notice how the rows of shingles slightly overlap and stack on top of each other. Be sure to leave a little basecoat color showing between each shingle to maintain the loose look of the roof. When painting the shingles on the stamp box, use the same technique, but switch to a no. 8 flat.

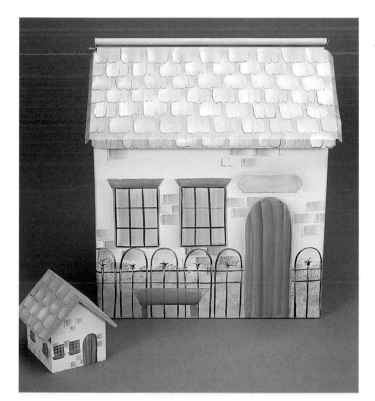

5 Using a 6/0 liner and slightly thinned Charcoal, loosely outline the left and lower edges of each roof shingle. Using a no. 16 flat and Tide Pool Blue, basecoat the door, window boxes and window headers. Basecoat the sign with Khaki Tan. Shade the lower edges of the window boxes and window headers using a no. 10 flat double loaded into Tide Pool Blue and Charcoal. Use the same brush mix and vertically streak the door to indicate wood slats. When painting the stamp box, use the same technique, but switch to a no. 4 flat or a no. 8 flat.

THE HOUSE DETAILS, WREATH *and* FOLIAGE

6 Using a 6/0 liner and slightly thinned Charcoal, paint thin vertical lines on the door to indicate woodgraining. Paint a few additional highlight wood grain lines in White. Using a no. 10 flat side loaded into White, highlight the top edges of the window headers, window boxes and the left edges of the wooden slats on the door. Shade the left side of the windows with a sheer side-load float of Charcoal. Using a 6/0 liner and White, paint several thin diagonal lines randomly over the window panes to indicate a shine on the window glass. Outline the windows with lines of Tide Pool Blue. Outline the door with a line of Charcoal. Shade the outside edges of the sign with a soft side-load float of Burnt Umber. Using a 6/0 liner and Tide Pool Blue, outline the sign. Highlight this outline with hit-and-miss short lines of White. Use the same technique to paint the stamp box, but switch to a no. 4 or no. 8 flat.

7 Using a 6/0 liner and slightly thinned Charcoal, paint the door hinges and door handle. Highlight hit-and-miss with lines of White. Paint the wreath on the door with circular, thin linework in the following layers of colors: Dark Burnt Umber, Khaki Tan, Raw Linen. Using a no. 8 flat double loaded into Charcoal and White, paint a horizontal stripe to indicate a door stoop. When painting the stamp box stoop, use the same technique, but switch to a no. 1 liner.

8 Using a no. 8 deerfoot and Dark Forest Green, lightly stipple foliage into all window boxes. Highlight this foliage with an additional light layer of Sea Grass. Using a no. 4 flat and Dark Forest Green, randomly paint small one-stroke leaves trailing from the window boxes. When painting the foliage in the stamp box, use a smaller deerfoot. Using a 6/0 liner, paint the bow on the wreath as loose linework of Wild Rose. Shade the bow next to the knot and where the ties pass under the bow loops with short lines of Deep Burgundy. Highlight the bow on the outside curves of the bow loops and on the curves of the ties with short lines of White.

THE FLOWERS, WISTERIA *and* WELCOME SIGN

10 Using a no. 4 flat double loaded into Wisteria and Purple Smoke, paint small dabs of color for the flower shapes in the window boxes. Paint the pink flowers using the same brush and technique with a double load of Deep Burgundy and Wild Rose, touched occasionally into White for a highlight. I like to trail a few blossoms down onto the window boxes to loosen the overall look of the flower display. Using the tip of a liner, paint the centers of the flowers with small dots of Pale Yellow. Use the tip of a liner to paint the flowers onto the foliage for the stamp box.

9 Using a no. 1 liner and slightly thinned Dark Burnt Umber, pull thick tree trunks into very thin branches on the sides of the mailbox and stamp box. Using a no. 1 liner and White, paint small one-strokes for the daisy flower shapes on top of the foliage in the window boxes. Dot the center of each daisy with Pale Yellow. Using a no. 8 deerfoot double loaded into Dark Forest Green and Sea Grass, touched occasionally into Raw Linen for a highlight, lightly stipple the ground foliage onto the mailbox and stamp box.

11 Using a no. 1 liner and Burnt Umber, pull the wisteria vine from the lower right edge on the front of the mailbox and stamp box loosely up the side and trailing onto the roof and front edge of the boxes. Using a no. 8 deerfoot and a double load of Dark Forest Green and Sea Grass, lightly stipple foliage on top of the vining and on the trees on the sides of the boxes. Using a no. 4 flat double loaded into Purple Smoke and Wisteria, paint small **C**-shaped strokes to form wisteria clusters along the vining. Using a 6/0 liner and Charcoal, print the "Welcome" lettering onto the sign above the door. Erase any visible pattern lines. Brush on two to three layers of J.W. Right Step Clear Varnish. Let cure twenty-four hours between coats.

Sturgeon Point Lighthouse Basket

As Michiganers, we are proud of the many different lighthouses we have. What better way to spend a day than packing a picnic basket and visiting one of the lighthouses and the wonderful scenery around it.

paint colors

(D) = Delta Ceramcoat Acrylics; (DA) = DecoArt Americana

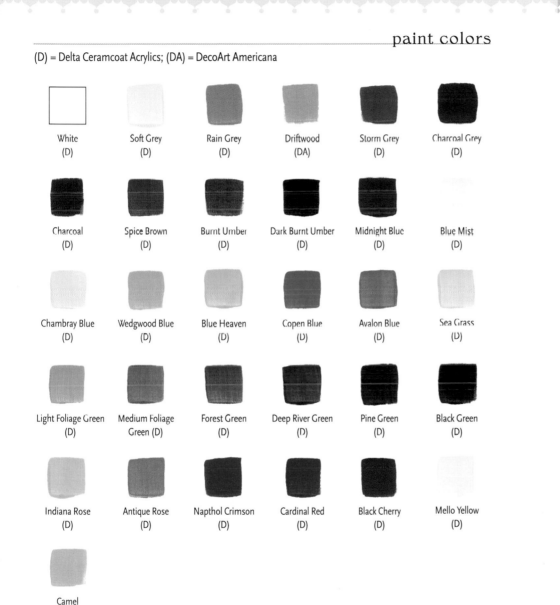

White (D)	Soft Grey (D)	Rain Grey (D)	Driftwood (DA)	Storm Grey (D)	Charcoal Grey (D)
Charcoal (D)	Spice Brown (D)	Burnt Umber (D)	Dark Burnt Umber (D)	Midnight Blue (D)	Blue Mist (D)
Chambray Blue (D)	Wedgwood Blue (D)	Blue Heaven (D)	Copen Blue (D)	Avalon Blue (D)	Sea Grass (D)
Light Foliage Green (D)	Medium Foliage Green (D)	Forest Green (D)	Deep River Green (D)	Pine Green (D)	Black Green (D)
Indiana Rose (D)	Antique Rose (D)	Napthol Crimson (D)	Cardinal Red (D)	Black Cherry (D)	Mello Yellow (D)
Camel (DA)					

materials

SURFACE

- Wood picnic basket from Pesky Bear, Machias, New York.

BRUSHES

- ¾-inch (19mm) and 1-inch (25mm) flats
- nos. 2, 4, 8, 12 and 16 flats
- no. 0 script liner and no. 1 liner

ADDITIONAL SUPPLIES

- small, round sponge
- satin acrylic varnish
- transparent tape
- stylus
- gray graphite paper

Pattern for Lighthouse Basket

This pattern may be hand-traced or photo-copied for personal use only. To return the pattern to full size you must first enlarge the pattern 200%, then enlarge that pattern 106%.

STAIN THE BASKET *and* TRACE PATTERN *on* THE LID

1 Stain the entire basket and lid with a mix of Blue Mist and satin acrylic varnish (1:1). This mix will go on as a stain and allow the wood graining to show through.

2 Trace the pattern on the lid with your stylus and gray graphite paper. The five straight lines are the foreground pine trees, not the pines in the background that fade away.

THE SKY

3 Wet the entire sky area with clean water. With a 1-inch (25mm) flat, wash down from the top edge with a soft float of Chambray Blue and Wedgwood Blue.

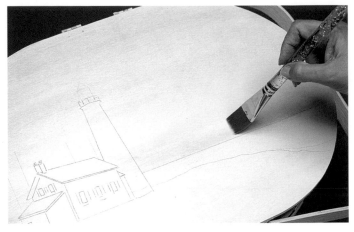

4 While it is still wet, wash up from the horizon line with Indiana Rose plus a touch of Antique Rose. Clean your brush and add a soft wash of Mello Yellow to break the color flow between the pinks and the blues.

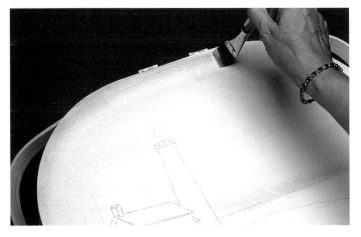

5 Allow the top to dry. With a side-load float of Blue Heaven on a 1-inch (25mm) flat, float around the top edge of the lid to frame the design.

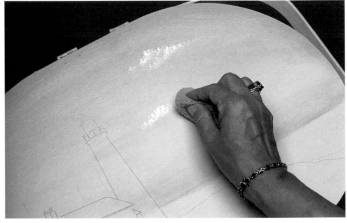

6 Slightly dampen a small, round sponge and touch into a little White. Sponge on the tops of the clouds and softly streak out the bottoms of the clouds.

7 With a 1-inch (25mm) flat side-loaded in Blue Heaven, softly streak under the clouds.

THE WATER

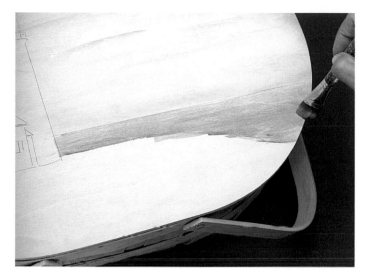

8 Wash over the entire water area with watery Blue Heaven. Deepen the color with Avalon Blue using a ¾-inch (19mm) flat.

9 Touch a corner of the brush into Copen Blue, and streak it into the water to add depth. Be careful that this color does not overtake the other water colors.

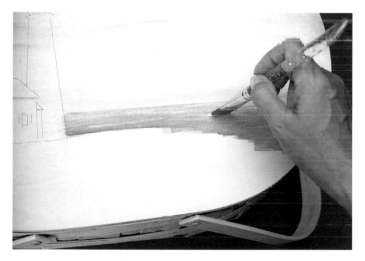

10 Corner load the ¾-inch (19mm) flat into White, and streak in some water movement.

11 Lightly add some tints of the Indiana Rose, Antique Rose and Mello Yellow. When you are painting reflective water, the water must contain all of the colors used in the sky.

PAINT THE GRASS, TREES *and* FOLIAGE

12 Wash in the ground with one coat of Forest Green using a 1-inch (25mm) flat.

13 Add some random tints and streaks of Medium Foliage Green, Sea Grass and Camel. Streak the Camel near the water to indicate sand along the edge of the water.

14 Wet the entire sky area where it meets the trees with clean water. Using a no. 12 flat, tap in the distant pine trees on the chisel edge of the brush with a double load of Deep River Green and Sea Grass. Since the background is wet, the trees should bleed a little and soften into the background. Change the colors of the trees by adding touches of Black Green to the dark side and Forest Green to the light side of the brush.

HINT ‣ *Before you begin painting, tape off the lighthouse and tops of the houses with transparent tape. Seal the edges of the tape with your finger to prevent the paint from bleeding under. This will keep your buildings clean, and you will not have to do as many layers of basecoat to clean them up.*

15 Using a no. 0 liner, paint the trunks of the trees with lines of Burnt Umber. Using a no. 12 flat and stippling on the chisel edge of the brush, tap in the tree branches with a double load of Forest Green into Pine Green on the dark side and Sea Grass on the light side. To vary the color of the trees, you may add Deep River Green to the dark side of the brush.

16 After the trees are dry, float a soft shadow of Black Green around the top of the house where the trees meet the roof, using a 1-inch (25mm) flat. This will slightly deepen the foliage and eliminate any negative light spaces that were left.

BEGIN THE LIGHTHOUSE

17 Remove all of the tape, and basecoat the lighthouse and house with Soft Grey using a no. 16 flat. Paint only the main pillar and the bottom half of the light fixture area of the lighthouse.

18 Shade the lighthouse and house with a side-load float of Rain Grey using a no. 16 flat. Shade the left side of each section of the house, under the windows, under the roofs and the left side of the lighthouse.

19 Highlight the right side of the house sections and lighthouse with White using a no. 16 flat. To help create the roundness of the lighthouse, float some reflected light along the edges of the lighthouse pillar. This moves the shade color away from the edge and rounds the object. Using a ¾-inch (19mm) flat and a very soft float of Soft Grey, float down both sides of the lighthouse.

20 Using a no. 8 flat, wash in the windows with a thin coat of Midnight Blue. Shade the left side of each window with a side-load float of Midnight Blue.

LIGHTHOUSE, *continued*

21 Basecoat the roofs of the main building with Rain Grey using a no. 16 flat. Shade with Storm Grey, starting at the tops of the roofs and working down.

22 Highlight the lower edges of the roofs with Soft Grey.

23 Create a foundation line on the buildings about ¼-inch (6mm) from the bottom with a side-load float of a mix of Rain Grey and Storm Grey, using a ¾-inch (19mm) flat. Base in the red trim around the windows, the shutters, window sills, lighthouse roof and the eaves under the roofs with Cardinal Red using the no. 1 liner.

24 Shade the red areas with Black Cherry using the no. 1 liner. Shade the shutters next to the windows with a no. 2 flat, but still leave a line of Cardinal Red for the window frame. Highlight the window frames and sills with a streak of Napthol Crimson using a no. 1 liner.

25 Outline the left and lower side of the two windows on the lighthouse with White. Softly shade next to the White with Rain Grey. Outline the main window of the lighthouse with White. Shade the roof with Black Cherry and highlight with Napthol Crimson.

26 Base the red railing in Cardinal Red, shade with Black Cherry and highlight with Napthol Crimson. Create the support beam under the railing with a line of White. Add the shine lines on the glass with fine lines of White. Use your no. 0 liner for each step.

27 Paint the chimney Soft Grey, shade with Rain Grey and highlight with White using a no. 4 flat. Paint the metal tops on the chimney with Black Cherry. Paint the supports under the railing with short lines of White using a no. 0 liner. Shade in between the supports with a brush mix of Rain Grey and Storm Grey using a no. 4 flat.

28 Thin Rain Grey with a little water and use a no. 4 flat to stroke under the roof lines. This will create the shadows from the roof overhang.

DRAW *the* BIRCH TREES

29 Stroke in the trunks and main branches of the birch trees with a brush mix of Driftwood and Charcoal Grey using a no. 1 liner.

30 Shade the left side of the trunks with a corner load of Dark Burnt Umber using a no. 12 flat.

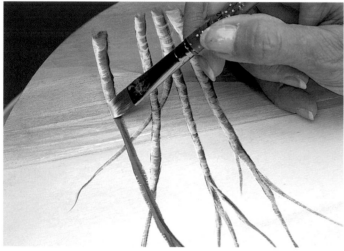

31 Stroke on the highlights on the birch bark with White using a no. 12 flat. Start with the chisel edge of the brush on the right edge of the tree trunk, and pull curved strokes inward toward the center to give the trunk a rounded appearance.

32 Add detail lines on the bark with Dark Burnt Umber using a no. 0 liner. Add a few more lines with White. Create the thin branches of the tree and bush branches with a brush mix of Dark Burnt Umber and Charcoal Grey using a no. 0 liner.

33 Slightly dampen a small, round sponge. Lightly sponge on Medium Foliage Green, then add touches of Light Foliage Green and touches of White to lighten the greens. Also add very light touches of Pine Green. Paint soft foliage on the tree at the base of the tree and on the bushes by the house and lighthouse.

THE PATH, SEAGULLS *and* CLOUDS

34 Streak in the path with washes of Spice Brown and Charcoal Grey. Add some soft streaky shading under the buildings, under the bushes and on the paths. Add touches of Forest Green and/or Pine Green to the browns to make a brownish-green for these shadows. Stipple or sponge some bushes on the lower left portion of the lid to soften the edge.

35 Using a ¾-inch (19mm) flat, side load into White and fluff in the tops of clouds around the sides of the basket. With the chisel edge of the brush, streak out the bottoms.

36 Add some seagulls on the basket and on the handles using a no. 0 liner and a brush mix of Rain Grey and Storm Grey. Start with a small letter **v**, add a dash across the bottom of the **v** for the body and pull the wings out from the top of the **v**. Highlight the tops of the wings with White. Highlight the top of the body with White. Shade the tips of the wings and lower edge of the body with Charcoal. To make some of the seagulls look like they are off in the distance, paint them in a light gray and make them smaller.

37 Allow the painting to dry completely, erase any visible tracing lines and varnish with three coats of satin acrylic varnish. Remember to varnish the inside of the basket. In case food spills, you will be able to wipe it off easier. Enjoy your picnic basket for many summers to come.

Country Lamp *and* Shade

This country lamp can work with the decor in many rooms. Nothing looks more welcoming than a white picket fence and an arbor gate leading to the front door of the house. I decorated the shade and the base with the same strokework trim.

paint colors

(D) = Delta Ceramcoat Acrylics; (DA) = DecoArt Americana

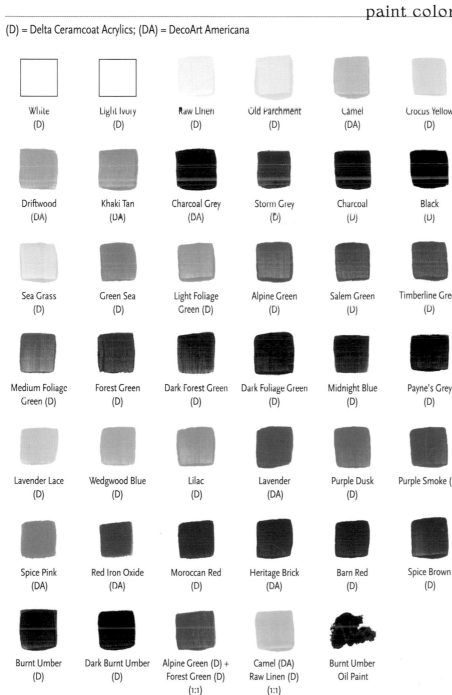

White (D)	Light Ivory (D)	Raw Linen (D)	Old Parchment (D)	Camel (DA)	Crocus Yellow (D)
Driftwood (DA)	Khaki Tan (DA)	Charcoal Grey (DA)	Storm Grey (D)	Charcoal (D)	Black (D)
Sea Grass (D)	Green Sea (D)	Light Foliage Green (D)	Alpine Green (D)	Salem Green (D)	Timberline Green (D)
Medium Foliage Green (D)	Forest Green (D)	Dark Forest Green (D)	Dark Foliage Green (D)	Midnight Blue (D)	Payne's Grey (D)
Lavender Lace (D)	Wedgwood Blue (D)	Lilac (D)	Lavender (DA)	Purple Dusk (D)	Purple Smoke (D)
Spice Pink (DA)	Red Iron Oxide (DA)	Moroccan Red (D)	Heritage Brick (DA)	Barn Red (D)	Spice Brown (D)
Burnt Umber (D)	Dark Burnt Umber (D)	Alpine Green (D) + Forest Green (D) (1:1)	Camel (DA) Raw Linen (D) (1:1)	Burnt Umber Oil Paint	

materials

SURFACE

- Lamp base by Wayne's Woodenware, Neenah, Wisconsin.

BRUSHES

- ¾-inch (19mm) and 1-inch (25mm) flats
- nos. 2, 4, 6, 8, 10, 14 and 16 flats
- no. 4 deerfoot stipple brush
- nos. 1 and 3 rounds
- no. 0 script liner

ADDITIONAL SUPPLIES

- lamp works kit
- lamp shade is available at Target Stores
- Minwax Ipswich Pine Wood Finish
- transparent tape — ¾-inch (1.9cm) wide
- small, round sponge
- old rag for antiquing
- Winsor & Newton Burnt Umber Oil Paint
- odorless mineral spirits
- pencil and ruler
- satin acrylic varnish
- stylus
- gray graphite paper

Patterns for Country Lamp Base

These patterns may be hand traced or photocopied for personal use only. Enlarge at
167% to return to full size.

BASECOAT THE SKY *and* HILLS

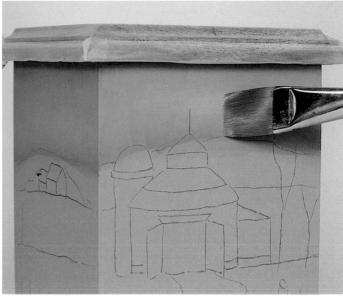

1 Stain the entire lamp base with the Ipswich Pine Wood Finish and let dry completely. Tape off the top and bottom of the lamp with transparent tape to keep the paint off. Basecoat the flat sides of the lamp with Wedgwood Blue and let dry completely. Tape around the bottom of the lamp, and trace on the pattern using your stylus and gray graphite paper. Use the tape line for the bottom of the fence.

2 Deepen the top of the sky, under the stained wood piece, with a side-load float of Purple Smoke using a 1-inch (25mm) flat. Softly float a mix of Purple Dusk + Lilac above the hill lines. Brush mix as you go around to get some variations of color in the sky. Soften these colors into the basecoat color of the sky.

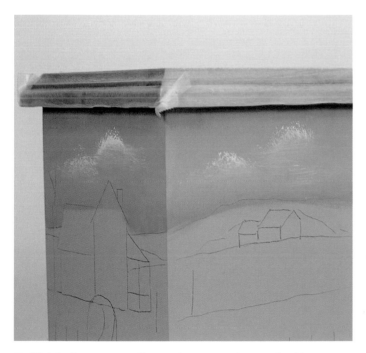

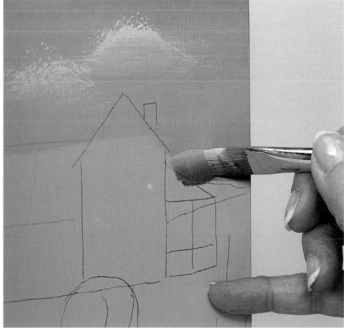

3 Slightly dampen a small, round sponge and corner load into White. Softly sponge on the top of the clouds and streak out the bottoms of the clouds.

4 Basecoat the back hill with Purple Smoke. Working wet-on-wet, double load a no. 14 flat with Dark Forest Green and Lavender Lace. Keep the tops of the hills very soft in color to help them fade into the distance.

HILLS, CROPS, TREES *and* FOLIAGE

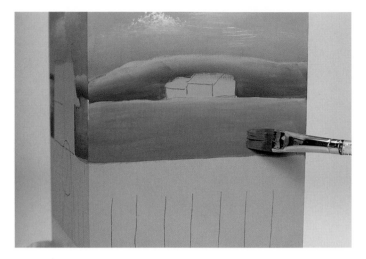

5 Basecoat the middle area with a mix of Alpine Green + Forest Green (1:1) using a no. 14 flat. Working wet-on-wet, highlight the tops of the hills with Sea Grass, and shade the bottoms of the hills with Timberline Green. Lightly streak the Timberline Green over the hills to add variation to the colors.

6 Use a very old no. 6 flat or a no. 3 round, and stipple in rows of crops. You can add Dark Foliage Green with any color of the greens already on your palette. Stipple the crops in slanted rows in the area between the round barn and the right side of the house.

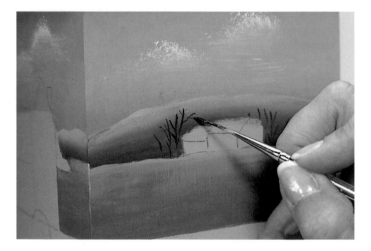

7 On the sides with the small buildings, paint the background trees with thin lines of Dark Burnt Umber and touch on Lavender Lace to lighten the tops. Use a no. 0 liner.

8 Start the foliage on these background trees with a soft stipple of Medium Foliage Green using a no. 4 deerfoot. Shade the base of the foliage with stipples of Dark Foliage Green and/or Dark Forest Green. Highlight the tops of the trees with Sea Grass, and/or Light Foliage Green touched into Wedgwood Blue, to blend the tops into the sky. Create the roads in this middle area with streaks of Timberline Green and Charcoal Grey. It may help to wet the area with clean water and then using a no. 4 flat, softly streak in the colors. Keep the streaks parallel to the horizon line.

ADD GRASS, PATHS *and* BASECOAT THE BUILDINGS

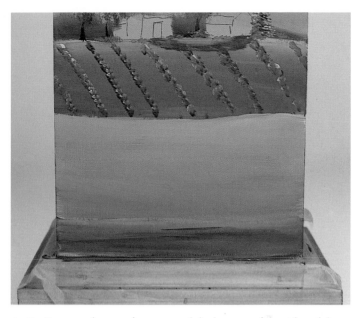

9 Solidly basecoat the front grass areas with Green Sea using a ¾-inch (19mm) flat. Highlight the tops with Sea Grass, and shade along the lower edge with Alpine Green.

10 Remove the tape from around the bottom of the sides of the lamp. Using a no. 10 flat, streak in the paths coming from the house and barn with a brush mix of Charcoal Grey, Burnt Umber, Driftwood and Charcoal. Keep the streaks parallel to the bottom of the lamp. Using a ¾-inch (19mm) flat double loaded into any combination of the browns and Green Sea, streak along the road at the bottom of the sides. This will help make a transition from the grass area to the road.

11 Use a no. 6 flat to basecoat the house near the red barn in Khaki Tan. Shade with Charcoal Grey and highlight with Raw Linen. Base the door and chimney with Barn Red and shade with Charcoal. Basecoat the barn with Barn Red, shade with Charcoal Grey and highlight with Moroccan Red. Paint both roofs with Charcoal highlighted with Raw Linen.

DETAIL THE BUILDINGS, STONES *and* FOLIAGE

12 Create the windows in the house and barn with Midnight Blue using a no. 2 flat. Outline around the windows, doors and roofs with Light Ivory. (White would be too bright for a building that far away.) Paint a picket fence with Raw Linen between the house and barn using a no. 0 liner. Lightly stipple the foliage around the base of the buildings with Dark Forest Green and Sea Grass using a no. 4 deerfoot.

13 Use a no. 6 flat to basecoat the house in Old Parchment, shade with Burnt Umber and highlight with Light Ivory. Paint the roof with Charcoal highlighted with Light Ivory, the door with Burnt Umber shaded with Charcoal and the chimney with Barn Red shaded with Charcoal. Using a no. 2 flat, add the windows in Midnight Blue. Use a no. 0 liner to outline all of the windows, the door and roof with Light Ivory. Create the foliage around the house and next to the path with Dark Foliage Green highlighted with Green Sea and Sea Grass using a no. 4 deerfoot. Stipple in the pine tree on the chisel edge of a no. 10 flat with a double load of Dark Forest Green into Green Sea plus a touch of Sea Grass.

14 Basecoat the red areas of the barn with Heritage Brick, shade with Payne's Grey and highlight with Red Iron Oxide using a no. 10 flat. Basecoat the roof of the barn, main section of the silo and stone foundation areas with Storm Grey. Basecoat the top of the silo with Driftwood. Shade the roofs on each side with Payne's Grey, and highlight in the center with Raw Linen.

15 Use a no. 2 flat to dab rocks on the silo and foundation with Driftwood, Raw Linen and Storm Grey. Touch your brush into any combination of these colors, and let them mix as you dab on the stones. Basecoat the barn door opening in Burnt Umber shaded on the right side with Black. Basecoat the yellow areas with Camel using a no. 1 round. Paint the lines on the silo roof with Payne's Grey using a no. 0 liner.

DETAIL THE HOUSE *and* BARN

16 Shade the Camel areas with Spice Brown, and highlight with a mix of Camel + Raw Linen (1:1). Use a no. 1 round for the small areas and a no. 8 flat for the doors. Paint the shingle lines on the roof with Payne's Grey using a no. 0 liner. Create the weather vane with Black.

17 Paint the windows with Midnight Blue using a no. 2 flat, and outline with fine lines of Camel using a no. 0 liner. Make stall boards on the inside of the barn door with lines of Driftwood shaded with touches of Black. Paint the straw with thin lines of Camel and Spice Brown. Using a no. 16 flat, shade the side of the building and the silo with a side-load float of Charcoal Grey plus a touch of Payne's Grey to set them back behind the main section of the barn. Use a no. 4 deerfoot to stipple the foliage around the base of the barn with Dark Foliage Green, Green Sea and Sea Grass.

18 Use a no. 16 flat to basecoat the house in Raw Linen, shade with Burnt Umber and highlight with Light Ivory. Use Charcoal highlighted with Light Ivory for the roof, and Salem Green shaded with a touch of Charcoal for the door. Paint the chimney with Barn Red shaded with Charcoal. Paint the tree trunk and branches with Burnt Umber with touches of Black.

19 Use a no. 2 flat to create the shutters and window boxes with Salem Green, and shade with a touch of Charcoal. Use Midnight Blue for the windows. Use a no. 0 liner to outline the windows, door, roof and porch railing with White. Paint the welcome sign with Khaki Tan, shade with Burnt Umber and tiny dashes of Burnt Umber to look like writing. Use a no. 0 liner for the light fixture in Crocus Yellow. Outline and crosshatch with fine lines of Black. Paint the siding lines with very thin lines of Burnt Umber. Softly shade the right side of the windows and doors with a side-load float of Burnt Umber and a no. 8 flat. Paint the porch floor with a line of Burnt Umber.

THE FOLIAGE, FLOWERS *and* FENCE

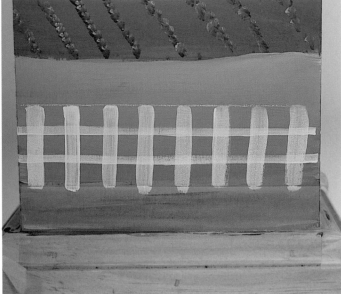

20 Use a no. 4 deerfoot to stipple the foliage in the window boxes and around the base of the house with Medium Foliage Green and highlight with Green Sea and/or Sea Grass. Stipple the pine tree in with a double load of Dark Foliage Green and Green Sea using the chisel edge of a no. 8 flat. Paint the foliage on the tree using Medium Foliage Green highlighted with Sea Grass. Make the flowers with dots of Spice Pink and White.

21 Retape the road along the bottom of the design to keep the bottoms of the fence neat, and retrace the fence pattern if needed. Basecoat the fence in Raw Linen. First paint the rails all around the lamp from one gatepost to another gatepost using a no. 2 flat. Use the no. 2 flat to paint the arbor with Raw Linen. Stroke in the pickets of the gate with a no. 4 flat and Raw Linen. Stroke in the pickets of the fence with a no. 6 flat.

22 Shade the pickets by pulling Charcoal Grey up from the bottom of each picket. Also, shade the railing to the right and left of the pickets with a soft float of Charcoal Grey using a no. 10 flat. This is darker on the right side of the picket and lighter on the left.

23 Highlight the pickets with White by pulling down from the top of each picket.

THE FENCE, VINING *and* FOLIAGE

24 Use a no. 0 liner to add a few wood graining lines with Charcoal Grey. To even out the tops of the pickets, add fine lines of White. Paint the ball finials of the posts with Raw Linen, shade with Charcoal Grey and highlight with White. Use lines of White for the molding trim under the finials.

25 Use a no. 0 liner with Dark Burnt Umber to paint thin, wiggly vines coming from each side of the arbor and over the top. Stipple the foliage in with a no. 4 deerfoot at the base of the vines and along the vines with lines of Medium Foliage Green highlighted with Sea Grass.

26 Paint the clematis with strokes of Lavender using a no. 0 liner. Add a dot of White for the center. Add some foliage around the base of the fence with Medium Foliage Green, Dark Foliage Green, Green Sea and Sea Grass. Stipple flowers on lightly with a no. 4 deerfoot using Crocus Yellow, Spice Pink, White, Moroccan Red or any other color you have on your palette.

OPTIONAL ♦ *You may add a small bush along the fence with branches of Burnt Umber with touches of Black. You can paint the foliage with any of the greens from your palette. You may add a vining rose bush on the fence with lines of Burnt Umber. Add foliage with the deerfoot in Medium Foliage Green and Sea Grass. Make the flowers using touches of Spice Pink and White. See the finished project on page 46.*

STROKEWORK TRIM

27 Remove all of the tape from the top and bottom of the lamp. Using a ruler, divide each side into four equal sections. Use a no. 3 round to paint long **S**-strokes with Burnt Umber.

28 Add two comma strokes below the **S**-stroke and one comma stroke above it. Add a dash between the ends of the **S**-strokes.

29 Draw a very faint pencil line 1¾ inches (4.5cm) from the bottom edge of the lampshade. Mark off every inch (2.5cm) along that line. Paint the same strokework trim design as on the base of the lamp.

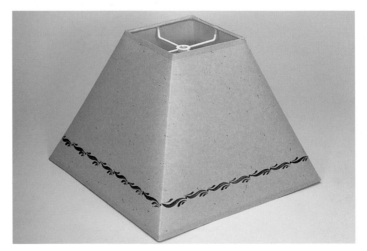

FINISHING TOUCHES

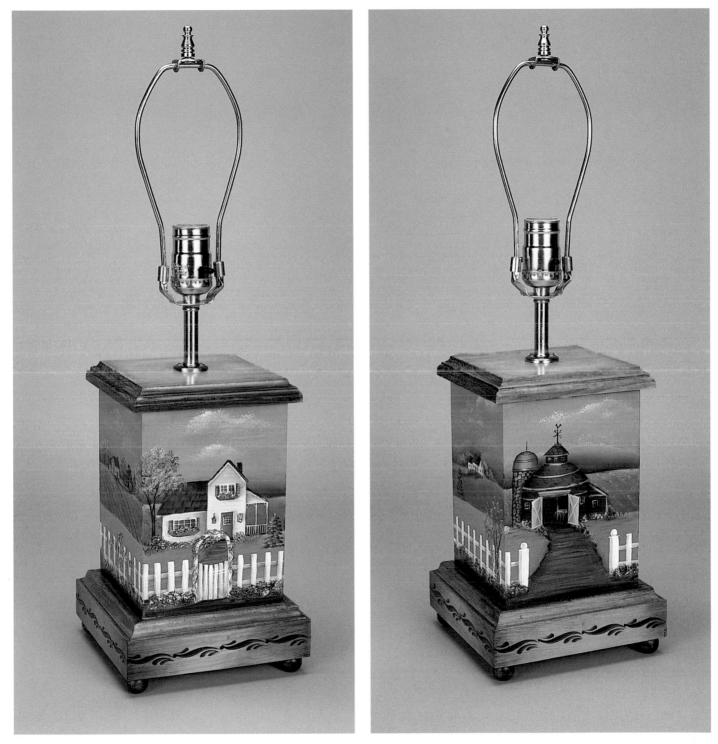

30 Allow the painting to dry completely and then erase any visible tracing lines. Varnish the entire lamp base with one coat of satin acrylic varnish. Dampen the stained areas of the base with a little mineral spirits. Apply a little Burnt Umber oil paint on a soft rag to the four corners of the bottom and top of the base. Gently blend the oil paint and spirits to soften the color. Allow the antiquing to dry twenty-four hours before adding two more coats of satin acrylic varnish. Wire the lamp with your lamp kit and enjoy.

Mitten Chest

What a lovely way to store those winter mittens and hats! Or place it next to your fireplace to hold kindling or newspapers for fire making. This cozy design will warm you all winter long.

paint colors

(D) = Delta Ceramcoat Acrylics; (DA) = DecoArt Americana

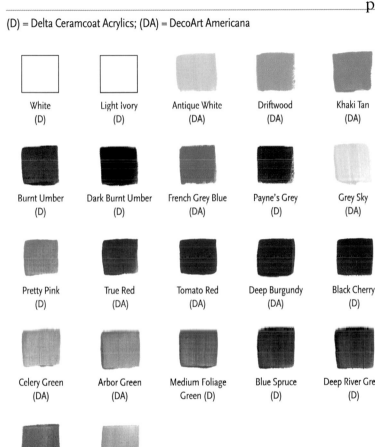

White
(D)

Light Ivory
(D)

Antique White
(DA)

Driftwood
(DA)

Khaki Tan
(DA)

Spice Brown
(D)

Burnt Umber
(D)

Dark Burnt Umber
(D)

French Grey Blue
(DA)

Payne's Grey
(D)

Grey Sky
(DA)

Charcoal
(D)

Pretty Pink
(D)

True Red
(DA)

Tomato Red
(DA)

Deep Burgundy
(DA)

Black Cherry
(D)

Lima Green
(D)

Celery Green
(DA)

Arbor Green
(DA)

Medium Foliage
Green (D)

Blue Spruce
(D)

Deep River Green
(D)

Black Green
(DA)

Blue Spruce (D)+
Celery Green (DA)
(1:1)

Lima Green (D) +
Celery Green (DA)
(1:1)

materials

SURFACE

- This wooden chest with a hinged lid is available from Wayne's Woodenware, Neenah, Wisconsin.

BRUSHES

- nos. 4, 8, 12 and 16 flats
- 1-inch (25mm) flat
- 6/0 and no. 1 liners
- no. 3 round
- no. 4 deerfoot stipple brush
- 1-inch (25mm) mop brush

ADDITIONAL SUPPLIES

- Minwax Ipswich Pine Wood Finish
- J.W. Right Step Clear Varnish, satin
- white graphite paper
- ruler and chalk pencil
- stylus

Patterns for Mitten Chest

These patterns may be hand-traced or photocopied for personal use only. Enlarge at
200% to return to full size.

BACKGROUND DETAILS *and* BUILDINGS

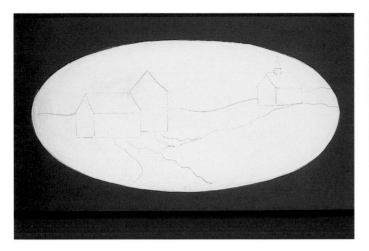

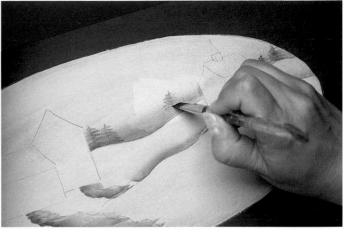

1 Stain the entire chest with Ipswich Pine Wood Finish. Let dry completely. Basecoat the base of the chest with Deep Burgundy. Using the outline of the holly pattern and a pencil, transfer the oval shape into the middle of the top of the lid. Basecoat the inside of the oval with Grey Sky. Basecoat the remainder of the lid with Blue Spruce. Let dry completely and sand lightly.

2 Side load a small amount of Payne's Grey on a 1-inch (25mm) flat, and softly shade at the horizon line to separate the two hill areas. Basecoat in the path areas on all three buildings with horizontal, streaky brushstrokes. Slightly dampen the surface with clean water. Using the chisel edge of a no. 12 flat loaded into Black Green, horizontally tap in the background pine trees. The moistened surface allows the background pine trees to softly bleed into the surface, giving the illusion of trees far in the distance… cool!

3 Using a 1-inch (25mm) flat side-loaded heavily into Light Ivory, side-load float mounds of clouds in the sky. Highlight the outside and/or top edges of the snow hills and along the edges of the paths using the side-loaded 1-inch (25mm) flat.

4 Using a no. 12 flat, basecoat the red house with Tomato Red. Shade to separate the red house sections with a side-load float of Black Cherry. Basecoat the middle house with Khaki Tan. Shade to separate the middle house sections with a soft side-load float of Burnt Umber. Basecoat the church with Antique White. Shade to separate the church sections with a side-load float of Spice Brown. Using a no. 4 flat, basecoat the chimneys with Tomato Red.

DETAIL THE BUILDINGS *and* ROOFS

5 Highlight the right side of each section of the red house with a side-load float of True Red using your no. 12 flat. Highlight the right side of the middle house with a side-load float of Antique White. Highlight the right side of the church front and steeple with a side-load float of White.

6 Use a stylus and white graphite paper to transfer the detail lines onto the houses. Using a no. 4 or no. 8 flat and Charcoal, basecoat all windows, the red house and the church doors. Basecoat the middle house door with Blue Spruce. Using a 6/0 liner and slightly thinned White, outline all windows and doors. Paint the doorknobs as dots of White.

7 Basecoat one roof at a time with Charcoal using a no. 12 flat. While the roof area is still wet, dip your dirty brush into White. Using the chisel edge of the brush, streak the White from the lower edge of the roof up into the roof area, lifting off the brush as you pull up.

8 Underline the roof areas with White using a 6/0 liner. Paint a horizontal line across the top edge of each chimney with linework of Charcoal.

BUSHES, SNOW *and* FENCE

9 Using a 1-inch (25mm) flat corner-loaded heavily into White, reinforce the highlight areas on the snow hills and edges of paths. Double load your no. 4 deerfoot into Black Green and Medium Foliage Green. Lightly stipple bushes at the base of the red and middle houses. Using an edge of the stipple brush, lightly streak across the lower edges of the bushes to blend them into the snow area.

10 Let the bushes completely dry. Then highlight the bushes with your no. 8 flat side-loaded into White to give the indication of snow on the foliage.

11 Using a no. 1 liner and slightly thinned Dark Burnt Umber, pull the thick tree trunks into very thin branches to form the bare trees. Highlight the tops and tips of some branches with linework of White to indicate snow on the branches. Paint all of the bare trees on the design, except the bare tree in the lower left corner of the oval insert.

12 Using a 6/0 liner and a loose double load of Burnt Umber into Driftwood, paint short vertical lines to form the fence posts and loose horizontal lines to indicate the fence railing. In front of the red house, notice how the fence posts are larger and spaced farther apart in the foreground area and get smaller and closer together as they fade into the background.

DETAIL THE FENCE *and* PINE TREES

13 Highlight the right side of the fence posts, and hit-and-miss along the top edge of the fence railings with linework in White.

14 Use a no. 8, no. 12 or no. 16 flat to paint the various sizes of pine trees. Double load the brush heavily with Black Green and Medium Foliage Green. Work on the chisel edge of the brush, and tap in the horizontal branches of the trees. Keep the Medium Foliage Green edge of the brush to the left side of each pine tree.

15 Using the dirty brush from painting the pine trees, tip one corner into White and lightly tap in the highlight on the left edge of each pine tree.

16 Make sure the pine trees are completely dry before applying the set-back shading. Use a no. 16 flat side-loaded into a small amount of Black Green, and float where the pine trees overlap to separate them from each other.

THE DOOR WREATHS *and* MAILBOX

17 Using the tip of a 6/0 liner, paint small dots in the following layers of colors to establish the round wreaths on the doors of all buildings: Deep River Green, Lima Green and True Red. Using a 6/0 liner loosely double-loaded into Charcoal and White, paint short horizontal lines to indicate the stoops along the lower edge of all doors. Using a no. 1 liner, paint the large bare tree in the lower left corner of the oval insert as instructed in step 11 on page 63.

18 Using a no. 8 flat, basecoat the mailbox with Antique White. Using a no. 4 flat, basecoat the mailbox post and supports with thick lines of slightly thinned Spice Brown. Using a 6/0 liner and slightly thinned Dark Burnt Umber, paint thin lines to indicate wood grain on the mailbox post and support. Basecoat the present with White.

19 Using a no. 8 flat, side-load float Spice Brown inside of the mailbox, at the base of the mailbox door and along the lower edge of the mailbox. When dry, reinforce these shade areas with an additional side-load float of Dark Burnt Umber. Highlight the curve of the mailbox door and the top edge of the mailbox with a side-load float of White. Using a 6/0 liner, outline the curves around the mailbox opening and mailbox door with a line of White.

DETAIL THE MAILBOX *and* HOLLY TRIM

20 Using a stylus, decorate the present with small dots of Deep River Green. Using a 6/0 liner and slightly thinned True Red, paint a loose bow and ties onto the present. Using a no. 4 flat, basecoat the mailbox flag with True Red. Shade across the lower edge of the mailbox flag with a side-load float of Black Cherry. Using a 6/0 liner brush, paint a line and dot of Dark Burnt Umber to indicate the flag support and rivet.

21 Side-load a 1-inch (25mm) flat into a small amount of Payne's Grey, and softly shade around the outside edge of the oval insert to set the scene into the oval shape. Also, reinforce the shading on the left side of the paths. Set the mailbox into the design by shading behind the mailbox, post and supports with a side-load float of Payne's Grey. Using a no. 1 liner and slightly thinned French Grey Blue, paint a line around the oval insert to enclose the design.

22 If you wish, you can dress up the oval insert with holly trim.

1. Using a no. 1 liner and slightly thinned Dark Burnt Umber, pull thick-lined branches to the thin tips of the branches. When the branches become very thin, pick up a little Khaki Tan on the brush to help the dark branches show up on the dark surface. Using a no. 8 flat, basecoat the holly leaves with Celery Green.

HINT ✦ *Hold the brush farther back on the handle than usual, and slowly twist it back and forth between your fingers as you pull the branches—they will automatically "kink and twist" for you!*

2. Using a no. 8 flat loaded with Khaki Tan, loosely overstroke the branches as far as you can go. When the branches become too thin to overstroke, tap the Khaki Tan onto the branches with the chisel edge of your brush. Messy is good. It looks like loose branch bark! Using a no. 8 flat, shade the base and partially down one side of each holly leaf with one to three layers of Deep River Green. Using a no. 4 flat, basecoat the berries with Tomato Red.

3. Load White onto a no. 8 flat, and paint a second layer of overstroke on the branches.

Again, overstroke as far as you can. When the branches become too thin to overstroke, tap the White onto the branches with the chisel edge of your brush. Highlight the opposite side of each holly leaf with a side-load float of Lima Green. Using a no. 4 flat, shade the half of each berry where it would be attached to the vining with a side-load float of Payne's Grey. Highlight the opposite side of each berry with a side-load float of True Red.

4. Paint thin, curved vein lines and side vein lines into each holly leaf using a 6/0 liner and a mix of Lima Green + Celery Green (1:1). Loosely outline the highlight side of each holly leaf with a thin line using the same brush mix. Using the tip of your liner brush, paint a dot of Pretty Pink on the high-light half of each berry. Using a no. 8 flat and a very sheer mix of Blue Spruce + Celery Green (1:1), paint sheer one-stroke leaves sparingly along the vining.

FINISH THE HOLLY TRIM *and* ADD STROKEWORK

23 Here, the holly trim is used on opposite corners of the oval to balance and fill out the design without overpowering the scene in the middle.

24 You can also dress up the base of the chest with some strokework trim.

1. Using a ruler and chalk pencil, mark a horizontal line 1½ inches (3.8cm) up from the lower edge of the chest. The scroll increments are spaced 2 ½ inches (6.4cm) apart.

2. Using a no. 1 liner and Arbor Green, paint the thin scroll lines—or as I call them, the strokework skeleton—between the 2½-inch (6.4cm) markings. Loosen the look of the strokework skeleton with thin lines ending in dashes of Arbor Green. Using a no. 8 flat and French Grey Blue, paint the long **S**-strokes at the base of each strokework skeleton curve.

3. Using a no. 3 round loaded heavily into French Grey Blue, paint large one strokes on either side of each **S** stroke on the border. Using a 6/0 liner and Grey Sky, paint very small one-strokes at the base of each strokework skeleton to unify the scroll design.

25 Brush on two layers of J.W. Right Step Clear Varnish using a 1-inch (25mm) mop brush. Let cure twenty-four hours and sand lightly between layers. Reattach hinges. Enjoy!

Bride's Box

One of the first designs we had for this book was this Bride's Box. When one of my daughters, a niece or nephew was getting married, I would paint him or her a Bride's Box. It is a wonderful keepsake the bride and groom can use to hold their remembrances from the showers, parties and the wedding. Our wedding is about to start, the bride is about to enter the church and everyone is waiting for her. Have fun painting this for the bride in your family.

paint colors

(D) = Delta Ceramcoat Acrylics; (DA) = DecoArt Americana

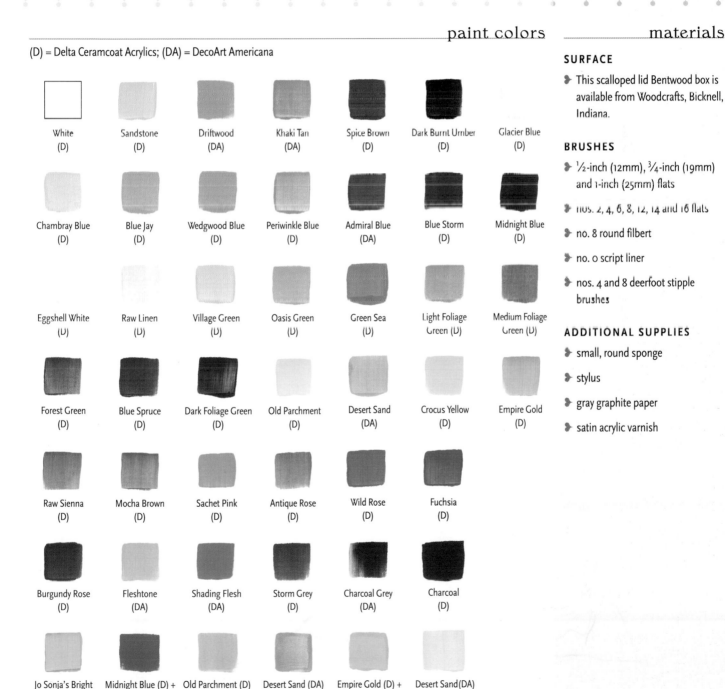

White (D)	Sandstone (D)	Driftwood (DA)	Khaki Tan (DA)	Spice Brown (D)	Dark Burnt Umber (D)	Glacier Blue (D)
Chambray Blue (D)	Blue Jay (D)	Wedgwood Blue (D)	Periwinkle Blue (D)	Admiral Blue (DA)	Blue Storm (D)	Midnight Blue (D)
Eggshell White (D)	Raw Linen (D)	Village Green (D)	Oasis Green (D)	Green Sea (D)	Light Foliage Green (D)	Medium Foliage Green (D)
Forest Green (D)	Blue Spruce (D)	Dark Foliage Green (D)	Old Parchment (D)	Desert Sand (DA)	Crocus Yellow (D)	Empire Gold (D)
Raw Sienna (D)	Mocha Brown (D)	Sachet Pink (D)	Antique Rose (D)	Wild Rose (D)	Fuchsia (D)	
Burgundy Rose (D)	Fleshtone (DA)	Shading Flesh (DA)	Storm Grey (D)	Charcoal Grey (DA)	Charcoal (D)	
Jo Sonja's Bright Yellow Wood Glaze	Midnight Blue (D) + Wedgwood Blue (D) (1:1)	Old Parchment (D) + Wild Rose (D) (3:1)	Desert Sand (DA) + Khaki Tan (DA) (1:1)	Empire Gold (D) + Old Parchment (D) (1:1)	Desert Sand (DA) + White (D) (1:1)	

materials

SURFACE

➤ This scalloped lid Bentwood box is available from Woodcrafts, Bicknell, Indiana.

BRUSHES

➤ ½-inch (12mm), ¾-inch (19mm) and 1-inch (25mm) flats

➤ nos. 2, 4, 6, 8, 12, 14 and 16 flats

➤ no. 8 round filbert

➤ no. 0 script liner

➤ nos. 4 and 8 deerfoot stipple brushes

ADDITIONAL SUPPLIES

➤ small, round sponge

➤ stylus

➤ gray graphite paper

➤ satin acrylic varnish

Patterns *for* BRIDE'S BOX

Lid

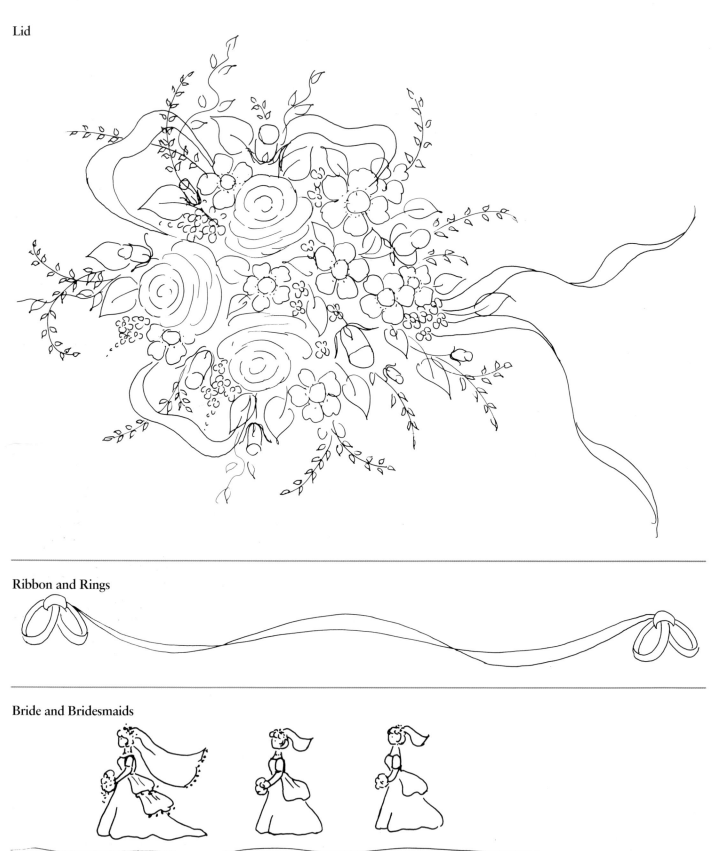

Ribbon and Rings

Bride and Bridesmaids

These patterns may be hand-traced or photocopied for personal use only. Enlarge the bouquet 185% to return to full size, the ribbon and rings 200% and the bride and bridesmaids 125%.

Houses

House and Church

These patterns may be hand-traced or photocopied for personal use only. Enlarge the houses 143% to return to full size and the house and church 125%.

BASECOAT THE LID *and* BEGIN THE BOUQUET

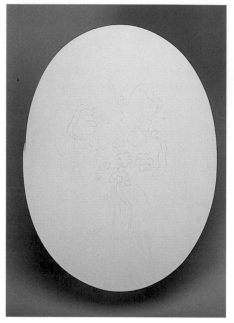

1 Basecoat the lid with a mix of Desert Sand + White (1:1). Sand between coats. Allow the basecoat to dry completely, then trace on the bouquet pattern with your stylus and gray graphite paper.

2 Slightly dampen a small, round sponge. Starting at the center of the bouquet design, softly sponge on the background. Start in the middle with Medium Foliage Green and work out to the edges of the design with the lighter colors of Green Sea and Village Green. Keep this soft so it will not overpower the design.

3 Double load a ½-inch (12mm) flat with Forest Green and Village Green plus a touch of Desert Sand added to the Village Green. Blend this double-loaded brush well on your palette, and stroke on the largest background leaves.

THE RIBBON

5 Use your ½-inch (12mm) flat to shade the ribbon with a side-load float of Wedgwood Blue. Shade the beginning of the streamers by the flowers, on either side of the turn in the ribbon, and in the center of the bow.

HINT ❥ *It is better to do these floats softly and repeat them than to try and get the shading done in one float. It makes for a softer and more natural look.*

4 Use a no. 8 flat to basecoat the ribbon with Chambray Blue.

6 Use a no. 14 flat to highlight the rises of the bow and any broad areas of the streamer with a flip-flop float of White.

7 Using a no. 0 liner, pull thin tendrils with a mix of Desert Sand + Khaki Tan (1:1). Use a no. 8 flat and the same mix for shadow leaves along the tendrils.

8 Use a no. 0 liner to pull long, graceful stems with a brush mix of Green Sea and Desert Sand. Use a no. 4 flat and the same mix to paint one-stroke leaves along the stems.

THE ROSES

9 Basecoat the rose circles with Antique Rose. Double load a no. 12 flat with Antique Rose and Wild Rose. Paint large **C**-strokes along the bottom of the rose and in the top third of the rose to create the rose's throat.

10 Double load a no. 12 with Antique Rose and White. Slightly ruffling the top of the stroke, paint the tops of the three circles inside of each other. If the white side of the brush starts to become pink, clean the brush and reload.

11 Use the white side of the double-loaded brush to complete the bottoms of the three circles. Start with the smallest and work toward the largest.

12 Stand the double-loaded brush on the chisel edge along the side of the rose.

13 Apply pressure to the brush, allowing the brush to slightly curve out.

14 Return to the chisel edge of the brush, and pull into the bowl of the rose.

15 Repeat with a petal on the other side and below the large petals. You may add small petals inside of the side petals as needed.

ROSES, *continued*

16 With the double-loaded no. 12 flat, do a **C**-stroke for the top of the rosebud.

17 Reverse the **C**-stroke to create the bottom petal of the rosebud.

18 For the calyx, use the no. 0 liner to pull irregular lines from the base of the bud with a brush mix of Medium Foliage Green and Forest Green.

19 With the same brush and color, add stems to the major leaves and the rosebuds.

20 Use the tip of the liner to add some White dots to the center of the roses and buds.

THE ANEMONES, BLUE FILLER FLOWERS *and* BABY'S BREATH

21 Use a no. 8 round filbert loaded with a mix of Old Parchment + Wild Rose (3:1). Tip the brush into White and pull the petals for the anemones.

22 Use a no. 6 flat to basecoat the anemone centers with Old Parchment. Shade the one side of the center with a float of Mocha Brown and highlight the other side with a float of White. Paint dots around the center with the same colors. Highlight some of the upper petals of the anemones with another float of White.

23 Use a no. 2 flat for the small **C**-strokes of the blue filler flower petals with a double load of White and Periwinkle Blue and/or Admiral Blue. Paint the centers using Old Parchment shaded with Wild Rose.

24 Use a no. 8 deerfoot and White to lightly stipple the baby's breath into any open areas in the design as filler. Add dots of White on top of the stippled area for detail.

THE RINGS *and* RIBBON

25 Basecoat the ribbon with Chambray Blue, shade with Wedgwood Blue and highlight with White. Basecoat the rings with Empire Gold and shade with Mocha Brown. Make the first highlight with a flip-flop float of a mix of Empire Gold + Old Parchment (1:1). Paint the second highlight with a flip-flop float of White. Glaze the rings with a thin wash of Jo Sonja's Bright Yellow Wood Glaze.

The finished lid

CLOUDS, HILLS *and* PATHS AROUND THE SIDES OF THE OVAL BOX

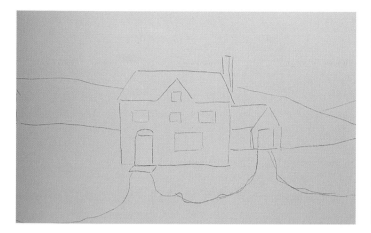

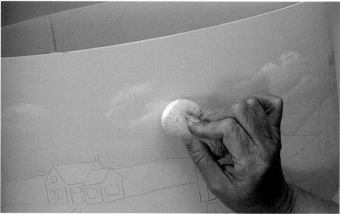

26 Basecoat the entire oval bentwood box, inside and out, with Chambray Blue. Sand between coats. Allow the paint to dry completely. Trace the designs for the houses and church around the sides of the box.

27 Use a 1-inch (25mm) flat to softly wash along the horizon line, and blend the sky area with a side-load float of Blue Jay. Follow along the trace lines of the tops of the hills and houses. Slightly dampen a small sponge and corner load it into White. Lightly sponge on the curved tops of the clouds, and softly streak out the bottoms.

28 Use a no. 16 flat to basecoat the back hills with Village Green. Shade the bottoms of the hills with Green Sea, and highlight the tops of the hills with Eggshell White. This is done wet-on-wet so you can blend these colors into each other.

29 Basecoat the pathways to the houses and along the bottom of the box with Driftwood. Use your ¾-inch (19mm) flat to shade along the edges of the paths of the road and pull streaks into the road with a double load of Driftwood into Spice Brown. Keep the streaks parallel to the bottom of the box.

30 Basecoat the front grass areas with Green Sea. Use a ¾-inch (19mm) flat to shade along the edges of the paths and the tops of grass areas with Medium Foliage Green.

FRONT GRASS AREA *and* CHURCH

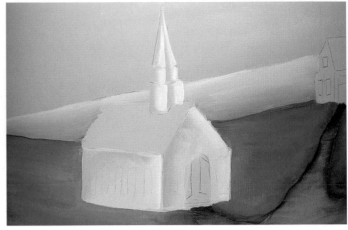

31 Use your no. 12 flat to deepen the shading of the paths below the doors with a side-load float of Charcoal Grey.

32 Basecoat the church with Raw Linen, shade with Sandstone and highlight with White.

33 Use a no. 2 and/or no. 4 flat to basecoat the windows and the open area of the door with Crocus Yellow. Shade on the left side of the windows with Raw Sienna. Paint the floor of the church in Spice Brown streaked with lines of Raw Linen. Basecoat the doors with Spice Brown and outline with Dark Burnt Umber. Use a no. 0 liner to outline the windows, door openings and crossbars on the windows in White.

34 Shade the church and steeple again with soft floats of Charcoal Grey. Use a no. 0 liner to paint the steeple railings in White. Paint the cross at the top with Crocus Yellow, and outline on the right side with fine lines of Raw Sienna.

THE PINK HOUSE

35 Use a no. 12 flat to basecoat the roof in Storm Grey. Shade the roof with Charcoal, beginning in the upper left corner and working down. Highlight with White starting at the lower right corner and working up. Use a no. 2 flat to add three steps in the front of the church door with a double load of Charcoal into White. Use your no. 0 liner to add a vine around the door with Dark Burnt Umber. Use a no. 4 deerfoot to add the foliage to the vine and along the base of the church. First lightly stipple in Dark Foliage Green, then high light with Light Foliage Green and Oasis Green.

37 Use a no. 12 flat to basecoat the house with Antique Rose. Shade the house with a double load of Antique Rose and Charcoal Grey. Blend this well on your palette to soften the gray. Highlight with a brush mix of Antique Rose and White. Paint the roof Charcoal highlighted with White.

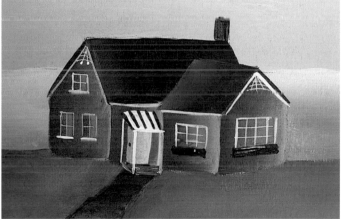

36 Paint straight lines of Dark Burnt Umber to indicate the trunks of the pine trees. Double load a no. 10 flat with Dark Foliage Green into Oasis Green and/or Light Foliage Green. Standing on the chisel edge of the brush, stipple in the horizontal branches, widening as you go down the tree. Use the tip of the liner or your stylus to add dots of flowers in the foliage around the church using Wild Rose and White. Add dots of Wild Rose in the vine around the door. Use a no. 0 liner to stroke in the fence with Sandstone, and highlight it with White.

38 Basecoat the door in Raw Linen and the awning in White with stripes of Burgundy Rose. Base the windows with a brush mix of Midnight Blue and Wedgwood Blue. Shade the left side with a float of Midnight Blue. Paint the window boxes and the chimney with Burgundy Rose and shade with a touch of Charcoal. Create the porch using Charcoal highlighted with White. Paint all of the trim lines around the windows, door, awning and under the roof with White using a no. 0 liner.

THE PINK HOUSE, *continued*

39 Paint the tree trunks and branches with lines of Dark Burnt Umber and Spice Brown, brush mixed for color variation. Use a no. 4 deerfoot for the foliage around the house and in the window boxes. Begin with Dark Foliage Green and then lighten with Light Foliage Green and Oasis Green. Dot flowers in this foliage with Wild Rose, Fuchsia and Periwinkle Blue.

40 Lightly stipple the tree foliage with Forest Green using a no. 8 deerfoot. Highlight the foliage with Green Sea and/or Oasis Green.

THE YELLOW HOUSE

41 Base the house with Old Parchment, shade with Spice Brown and highlight with White. Paint the roof using Charcoal highlighted with White. The chimney is Burgundy Rose shaded with Charcoal. Create the front door using Blue Spruce and the front steps with a double load of Charcoal into White using a no. 2 flat.

42 Base the windows with a mix of Midnight Blue + Wedgwood Blue (1:1). Shade the windows on their left sides with Midnight Blue. Use Blue Spruce for the shutters, window boxes and garage door. Use White for all of the trim lines.

THE BLUE HOUSE

43 Use a brush mix of Dark Burnt Umber and Spice Brown for the trees. Paint the foliage around the base of the house, on the tree and along the bottom of the box by the road with Dark Forest Green. Highlight with Light Foliage Green and/or Oasis Green using a no. 4 deerfoot. Create the pine tree using the same technique as in step 36 on page 81.

45 Using a no. 16 flat, basecoat the house with Wedgwood Blue, shade with Blue Storm and highlight with White. Paint the roof using Charcoal highlighted with White and the chimney using Burgundy Rose shaded with Charcoal. Use Antique Rose shaded with Burgundy Rose for the door. Paint the stairs with a no. 2 flat of Charcoal double-loaded into White.

44 Paint the dot flowers by the house with Fuchsia, Antique Rose and White. Create daisies by the road with strokes of White and centers of Crocus Yellow with White. Make the black-eyed Susans with strokes of Crocus Yellow with centers of Spice Brown. Paint the coneflowers using strokes of Wild Rose with Spice Brown cone-shaped centers. Use **C**-strokes of Periwinkle Blue and White for the delphiniums.

46 Base the windows in Wedgwood Blue + Midnight Blue (1:1). Shade their left sides with Midnight Blue. Paint all of the trim lines around the windows, door and under the roof with White. Use a brush mix of the Dark Burnt Umber and Spice Brown for the branches and tree trunks.

THE BLUE HOUSE, *continued*

BRIDE *and* BRIDESMAIDS

47 Paint the foliage around the base of the house and on the trees using Dark Forest Green highlighted with Light Foliage Green and Oasis Green. Use a no. 4 deerfoot. Make the dot flowers with Fuchsia and Crocus Yellow.

49 Trace on the pattern. Base the faces and arms with Fleshtone and shade with Shading Flesh. Paint the bride's hair using Crocus Yellow with touches of Raw Sienna. Give one bridesmaid Spice Brown hair. Add a touch of Dark Burnt Umber to the Spice Brown to create a darker look for the other bridesmaid's hair. Base the bride's dress in one sheer coat of Glacier Blue. Create the first bridesmaid's dress with one coat of Wild Rose and the next dress with one coat of Sachet Pink.

48 Using a no. 0 liner, paint the fence and arbor with Sandstone highlighted with White. Create the vine on the arbor with fine lines of Dark Burnt Umber. For the foliage, stipple lightly with Dark Foliage Green and Light Foliage Green. Add dots of Fuchsia and White for the roses.

50 Use a side-load float of White on a no. 4 flat for all of the folds and details of the bride's dress and veil. Add dots of White to the bottom of the veil, bustle and around her neck for pearls. Highlight the first bridesmaid's dress with side-load floats of Wild Rose and White. Highlight the next bridesmaid's dress with side-load floats of Sachet Pink and White. Dot on the bridesmaids' headbands with colors from their dresses. Stipple the bouquets first with Dark Forest Green. Create the bride's bouquet with both pink color dots and white dots. Give the bridesmaids' bouquets just two colors of pink dots.

THE COMPLETED BRIDE'S BOX

51 Allow the paint to dry thoroughly. Erase any visible tracing lines and varnish with at least three coats of your favorite satin acrylic varnish. If you are planning to give this as a gift, consider lining the inside of the bottom of the box. You can also personalize the gift with the name of the bride and your name painted on the inside of the lid of the box.

Back of box

Halloween Tote

*Add extra delight to your next Halloween celebration with this darling tote! It is tra-
ditionally filled with candy for trick-or-treaters, but how about using it for a fall floral
arrangement, as a serving piece for dry snacks or for a baby's first Halloween ven-
ture? In any case, it's such a fun piece to paint that you will be smiling long past
October 31st!*

paint colors

(D) = Delta Ceramcoat Acrylics; (DA) = DecoArt Americana

White (D)	Driftwood (DA)	Milk Chocolate (DA)
Dark Burnt Umber (D)	Yellow Ochre (DA)	Opaque Yellow (D)
Storm Grey (D)	Charcoal (D)	Black (D)
Medium Foliage Green (D)	Dark Forest Green (D)	Black Green (D)
Tangelo Orange (DA)	Cadmium Orange (DA)	Rookwood Red (DA)
Cape Cod Blue (D)	Purple Smoke (D)	Payne's Grey (D)

materials

SURFACE

❧ This Bentwood tote measuring 9" x 5" (22.5cm x 12.7cm) is available from Designs by Bentwood, Thomasville, Georgia.

BRUSHES

❧ nos. 4, 8, 10, 12 and 16 flats

❧ ¾-inch (19mm) and 1-inch (25mm) flats

❧ no. 6/0 liner

❧ no. 8 deerfoot stipple brush

ADDITIONAL SUPPLIES

❧ black Micron Pigma pen (optional)

❧ white graphite paper

❧ stylus

❧ transparent tape

❧ satin acrylic varnish

Patterns for Halloween Tote

These patterns may be hand-traced or
photocopied for personal use only. Enlarge
at 167% to return to full size.

THE BASECOAT, HORIZON LINE *and* HILLS

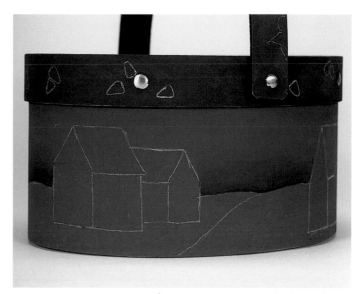

1 Basecoat the lower portion of the Bentwood tote with Purple Smoke. Basecoat the handle and rim of the tote with Charcoal. Using a stylus and white graphite paper, lightly transfer the main lines of the pattern onto the tote.

2 Using a 1-inch (25mm) flat brush side loaded into Payne's Grey, softly shade above the horizon line. The softened edge of color fades into the sky area.

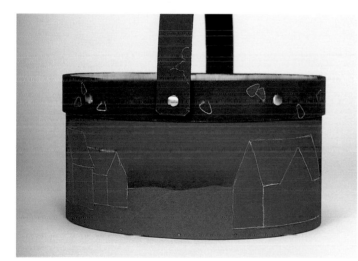

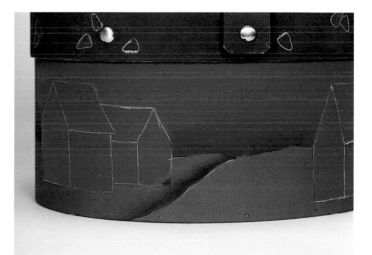

3 Basecoat all hills in Dark Forest Green using a ¾-inch (19mm) flat brush.

4 Side load Black Green on a ¾-inch (19mm) flat and softly shade to separate the hill sections.

HILLS, TREES *and* SHED

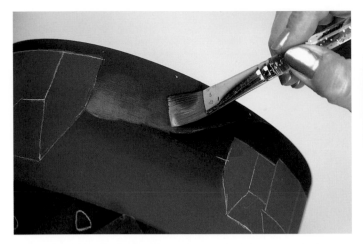

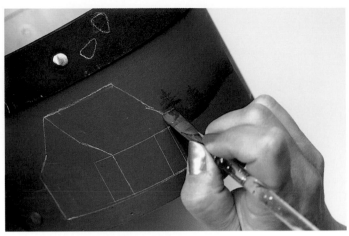

5 Use the ¾-inch (19mm) flat to moisten the hill areas with clean water. Next, side load your brush into Medium Foliage Green, and paint a smudgy or rough side-load float across the top of the hills of the slightly dampened surface. The small amount of moisture on the surface will diffuse and soften the Medium Foliage Green into the surface.

6 Use a no. 10 flat double loaded into Dark Forest Green and Black Green to paint the pine trees. Working on the chisel edge of the brush, horizontally tap in the pine tree branches.

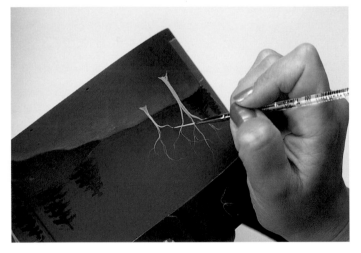

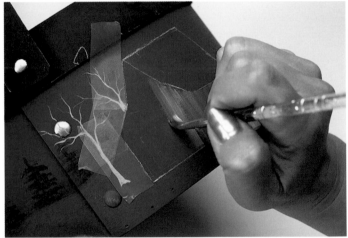

7 Use a 6/0 liner and slightly thinned Driftwood to paint the bare trees. I prefer to pull the trees from the thicker trunk into the very thin branches by holding my surface upside down and pulling the brush toward me. Loose is good!

8 Basecoat the shed streakily using a no. 8 flat loosely double loaded into Driftwood and Charcoal.

HINT ❥ *Make it easy for yourself by taping off the outside edges of the shed with transparent tape. It really makes it easy to keep your edges straight.*

DETAIL THE SHED *and* ROOFS

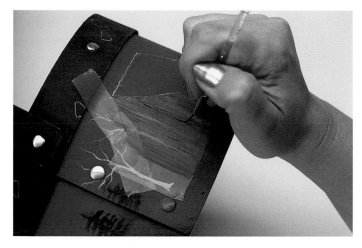

9 Using a 6/0 liner and slightly thinned Dark Burnt Umber, paint random thin, vertical lines on top of the shed basecoat to indicate wood grain lines.

10 Using a stylus and white graphite paper, transfer the details onto the pumpkin shed. Using a no. 8 flat and Black, basecoat the windows and door areas. With a no. 12 flat brush side loaded into Dark Burnt Umber, softly shade under the roof line and separate the shed sections.

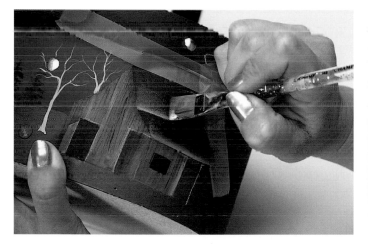

11 Tape off the background to keep the roof edges neat. Use a no. 16 flat to basecoat the roof in Black. While still wet, highlight the roof by picking up a little White on the corner of the Black-loaded brush. Blend the colors together on your palette, then horizontally streak across the lower edges of the roof.

12 Outline the roof, porch, window and door with a 6/0 liner and slightly thinned White.

SHED, FOLIAGE, GHOST *and* PUMPKINS

13 Side load White on a no. 16 flat, and highlight the outside edges of the shed and door with a soft side-load float.

14 Using a no. 8 flat and Black Green, horizontally side-load float along the outside edges of the path, and sparingly streak the Black Green horizontally through the path. Use a no. 8 deerfoot double loaded into Black Green and Medium Foliage Green to softly stipple in the foliage around the base of the shed. Keep the Medium Foliage Green side of the brush to the top of the bushes to indicate the highlight.

15 Paint small ovals of Cadmium Orange with a no. 4 flat for the pumpkins. Shade on one side with a side-load float of Rookwood Red, and highlight on the opposite side with a side-load float of Tangelo Orange. Use a liner brush to paint the stems as short lines of Medium Foliage Green. Loosely basecoat the ghost with a thinned White using a no. 4 flat. Use the tip of the 6/0 liner to paint small Black dots for the eyes.

16 Side-load float a small amount of Black Green on a no. 16 flat. Horizontally streak shading under the pumpkins and all of the trees to set them into the design.

THE YELLOW *and* BLUE HOUSES

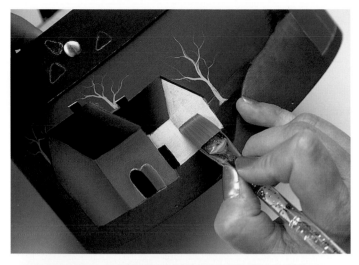

17 Basecoat the yellow house in Yellow Ochre with a no. 16 flat. Shade to separate the house sections and under the roof line with a no. 16 flat brush side loaded into a mix of Milk Chocolate plus a touch of Dark Burnt Umber. Basecoat the blue house with Cape Cod Blue. Shade to separate the house sections and under the roof line with a side-load float of a mix of Payne's Grey plus a touch of Dark Burnt Umber. Basecoat the roofs with Black. Highlight the right edges of the roofs with a soft side-load float of Black touched into White. Blend well on your palette before applying the edges of the roofs. Paint the chimneys with Black and the top with a line of White. Base the doors with Black.

18 Use a stylus and white graphite paper to transfer detail lines onto the houses. Basecoat the windows with two coats of Opaque Yellow using a no. 8 flat. Shade across the top of each window with a side-load float of Cadmium Orange.

19 Outline all windows in slightly thinned Black with a 6/0 liner. Dampen each window with a scant amount of clean water. Using a no. 4 flat, dab a little White behind the candle flame area and let it soften into the surface as the water diffuses the paint.

HINT ✦ *Paint all vertical lines on your windows first, then go back and paint all your horizontal lines.*

THE CANDLES, GHOST, PATHS *and* FOLIAGE

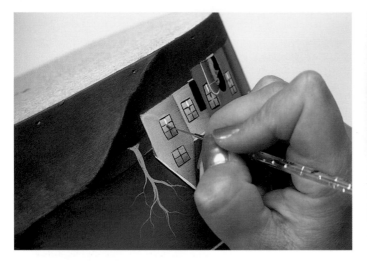

20 Paint a line of White with a 6/0 liner to indicate the candle-stick. Using the same brush, paint the flames as small one-strokes of Cadmium Orange. Outline the roof, door and steps with the liner and slightly thinned White.

21 Paint the ghost with a sheer layer of White and the eyes with dots of Black. Use a no. 8 flat and thinned Driftwood to wash in the horizontal path areas. Softly shade to the left side of each path with a side-load float of Charcoal.

22 Using a no. 8 deerfoot double loaded into Dark Forest Green and Tangelo Orange, lightly stipple in bushes along the base of the houses and paths. Make sure to keep the Tangelo Orange edge of the brush to the top of the bushes.

23 Paint the bare tree in front of the blue house using your liner and slightly thinned Dark Burnt Umber. Set the tree into the design by softly shading horizontally across the base of the bare tree with a side-load float of Black Green.

THE HAUNTED HOUSE *and* MOON

24 Basecoat the haunted house with Storm Grey using a no. 12 flat. Basecoat the roof with Black. Using a liner and slightly thinned Black, paint thin horizontal siding lines on top of the house. Using a no. 16 flat side loaded into Charcoal, softly shade to separate the house sections and under the roof line.

25 Using a no. 12 flat side loaded sparingly into White, softly highlight the edge of the door and house.

26 Transfer the details onto the house using a stylus and white graphite paper. Use a no. 8 flat to basecoat the yellow windows and door with two coats of Opaque Yellow. Softly shade across the top of each window and on the right side of the door with a side-load float of Cadmium Orange. Using no. 8 flat, basecoat the green window with a mix of Medium Foliage Green plus a touch of Opaque Yellow. Shade across the top of the window with a side-load float of Dark Forest Green. Use the same brush to basecoat the moon with one layer of Opaque Yellow. Shade the right side of the moon with a smudgy side-load float of Cadmium Orange.

27 Using a 6/0 liner and slightly thinned Cadmium Orange, outline each window, door and door opening. Using a no. 4 flat and Cadmium Orange, basecoat the shutter next to the green window. Paint a thin line of Cadmium Orange under the roof edge.

THE GHOSTS, PUMPKINS, FOLIAGE *and* BANNER

28 Paint a sheer ghost peeking out of the window using a no. 4 flat and slightly thinned White. Use the tip of your liner to paint Black dot eyes on the ghost. Using the 6/0 liner, basecoat the witch and cat with Black. Paint the pumpkin in the window as a small oval of Cadmium Orange, shade on one side with a side-load float of Rookwood Red and highlight on the opposite side with a side-load float of Tangelo Orange. Using a no. 8 flat, wash in the path area with streaky, horizontal strokes of Driftwood. Shade on the left side of the path with a side-load float of Charcoal.

29 Using a no. 4 flat and very sheer White, streak in the "boo" banner.

30 Using a 6/0 liner, paint shading lines of Black on the banner. Use the same liner and thinned White to outline and highlight the banner. Paint the lettering "Boo-Boo" onto the banner using the liner and Black.

HINT ❥ *If you are not comfortable with small detail lines, use a Micron Pigma pen...it's a lot easier!*

31 Double load a no. 8 deerfoot into Medium Foliage Green and Tangelo Orange. Softly stipple foliage along the base of the haunted house. Keep the Tangelo Orange side of the brush to the top of the foliage to indicate the highlight on the bushes. Using the no. 8 flat double loaded into Black Green and Dark Forest Green, horizontally stipple the small pine trees in front of the haunted house.

THE GRAVESTONES

32 Basecoat the gravestones with a no. 4 flat and thinned Driftwood. Using a no. 8 flat side loaded into a small amount of Charcoal, shade along one side—just in from the outside edge—on each gravestone.

33 Detail the gravestones with thin linework using a 6/0 liner and thinned White. Using a no. 8 flat corner loaded sparingly into Black Green, softly shade horizontally under the bottom of each gravestone to sink them into the design.

THE CANDY CORN *and* GHOSTS

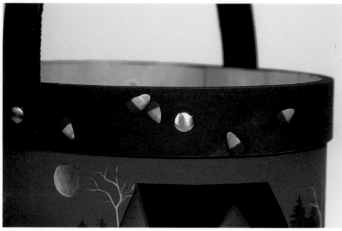

34 Using a no. 4 flat, basecoat each candy corn with White. Paint the orange sections with Cadmium Orange, the yellow section with Opaque Yellow and the white section with an additional layer of White.

35 Using a no. 8 flat brush side loaded into a small amount of Payne's Grey, softly shade the lower edge of each candy corn to separate any overlapping pieces.

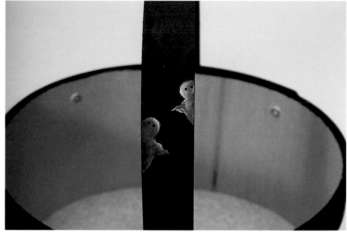

36 Using a 6/0 liner and White, paint a short stroke down the side of each candy corn, just opposite of the shaded side.

37 Decorate the handle with more scary ghosts! Basecoat the ghosts with a sheer layer of thinned White using a no. 4 flat. Paint dot eyes using the tip of your liner and Black.

FINISHING TOUCHES

38 Erase any visible pattern lines. Varnish to protect your painting with two to three layers of acrylic varnish. Let cure twenty-four hours and sand lightly between coats. Fill with candy and hope you don't have too many trick or treaters.

Four Seasons Recipe Box

These drawers will hold 4" × 6" (10.2cm × 15.2cm) recipe cards, but don't just limit this piece to a recipe box. It can also be used as an office center—holding paper clips, rubber bands, stamps, push pins, etc. The house is painted identically on all four drawers. Change the foliage to indicate the seasons. This is fun and easy to paint!

paint colors

(D) = Delta Ceramcoat Acrylics; (DA) = DecoArt Americana

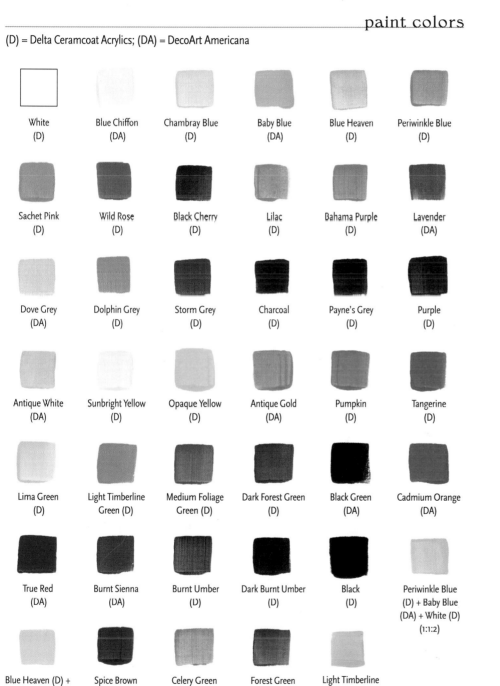

White (D)	Blue Chiffon (DA)	Chambray Blue (D)	Baby Blue (DA)	Blue Heaven (D)	Periwinkle Blue (D)
Sachet Pink (D)	Wild Rose (D)	Black Cherry (D)	Lilac (D)	Bahama Purple (D)	Lavender (DA)
Dove Grey (DA)	Dolphin Grey (D)	Storm Grey (D)	Charcoal (D)	Payne's Grey (D)	Purple (D)
Antique White (DA)	Sunbright Yellow (D)	Opaque Yellow (D)	Antique Gold (DA)	Pumpkin (D)	Tangerine (D)
Lima Green (D)	Light Timberline Green (D)	Medium Foliage Green (D)	Dark Forest Green (D)	Black Green (DA)	Cadmium Orange (DA)
True Red (DA)	Burnt Sienna (DA)	Burnt Umber (D)	Dark Burnt Umber (D)	Black (D)	Periwinkle Blue (D) + Baby Blue (DA) + White (D) (1:1:2)
Blue Heaven (D) + White (D) (1:1)	Spice Brown (D)	Celery Green (DA)	Forest Green (D)	Light Timberline Green (D) + White (D) (1:1)	

materials

SURFACE

❧ Four-drawer recipe box, measuring 5 ½"x 11"x 17" (14cm x 27.9cm x 43.2cm), is available from Wayne's Woodenware, Neenah, Wisconsin.

BRUSHES

❧ nos. 2, 4, 8, 10 and 12 flats

❧ 1-inch (25mm) flat

❧ nos. 4 and 8 deerfoot stipple brushes

❧ 6/0 and no. 1 liners

ADDITIONAL SUPPLIES

❧ transparent tape

❧ Minwax Ipswich Pine Wood Finish

❧ stylus

❧ white graphite paper

❧ satin acrylic varnish

Pattern for Four Seasons Recipe Box

This pattern may be hand-traced or photocopied for personal use only. Pattern is shown at full size. Use this pattern
for all four drawers. For the winter drawer, add a snowman (see page 108 for details).

BASECOAT THE DRAWERS

1 Stain the entire recipe box with the
Ipswich Pine Wood Finish. Let dry completely. Basecoat the drawer fronts to correspond to the season you will paint on them.
Starting in the upper left corner, basecoat the
spring drawer with Blue Chiffon. In the
upper right corner, basecoat the summer
drawer with a mix of Periwinkle Blue + Baby
Blue + White (1:1:2). In the lower left corner,
basecoat the autumn drawer with a mix of
Blue Heaven + White (1:1). In the lower right
corner, basecoat the winter drawer with
Chambray Blue. Using a stylus and white
graphite paper, transfer the pattern onto each
drawer.

HILLS, STONE FOUNDATION WALLS *and* SIDING

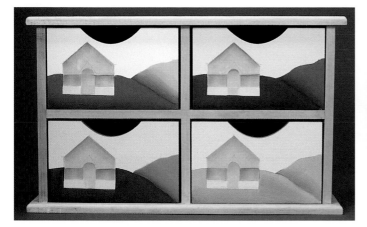

2 Basecoat the house—it is painted identically on all four drawers—with one layer of Antique White. You should still be able to see the pattern through the basecoat. Using a no. 12 flat side-loaded into Burnt Umber, softly shade the outside edges and under the roof lines of each house. Basecoat the stone foundation wall with Dove Grey. For the spring drawer, basecoat the back hill with a mix of Light Timberline Green + White (1:1), and the foreground hill with Medium Foliage Green. Use a no. 12 flat to shade the lower edge of the front hill with a side-load float of Dark Forest Green. On the summer drawer, basecoat the back hill with Medium Foliage Green and the foreground hill in Dark Forest Green. Use a no. 12 flat to shade the lower edges of both hills of the summer drawer with a side-load float of Black Green. For the autumn drawer, basecoat the back hill with Antique Gold and the foreground hill with Dark Forest Green. Use a no. 12 flat to shade the lower edge of the back hill with a side-load float of Dark Forest Green. Shade the lower edge of the front hill with a side-load float of Black Green. Base all hills on the winter drawer with Dolphin Grey. Use a no. 12 flat side-loaded into a small amount of Payne's Grey to shade the lower edge of both hills.

3 Use a no. 10 flat and Black to basecoat the door and windows. Use a no. 8 flat and White, and side-load float a highlight on the curve of the porch. To paint the stones, use a no. 4 flat loosely double loaded into Storm Grey and White to randomly smudge in oval shapes. Use a no. 10 flat side-loaded into Burnt Umber, and shade to the left of each window to set them into the design.

4 Outline the door and windows with thinned White using a 6/0 liner. Paint a dot of White to indicate a doorknob, and vertical lines of White for the pillars on the porch. Use your liner and thinned Charcoal to loosely outline each stone in the wall.

5 Use a no. 1 liner and Black to outline the two roof areas. With the same liner, paint a line of Storm Grey across the top of the stone wall to indicate a stone ledge. Next, use a 6/0 liner and thinned Burnt Umber to paint thin horizontal siding lines onto the house.

SPRING

6 Using a no. 4 deerfoot double loaded into Dark Forest Green and Lima Green, softly stipple rows of crops curving down the background hill. Moisten the surface with clean water. Stipple in some light background trees with a brush mix of Dark Forest Green and Lima Green. Pull faint lines to indicate tree trunks into the background tree area with a 6/0 liner and thinned Spice Brown. Moisten the surface and highlight the top edge of the front hill with your no. 8 deerfoot and Light Timberline Green.

7 Using a no. 8 deerfoot, stipple curves of White for the clouds. Paint the fence posts and fence railings with a no. 1 liner loosely double loaded into Dolphin Grey and White. Using your same liner and thinned Dark Burnt Umber, pull thin, loose lines to form the tree trunks and branches. Using a no. 8 flat and Dark Burnt Umber, side-load float in the path leading to the house. Using the no. 1 liner double loaded into Storm Grey and White, paint short horizontal stripes for the steps leading to the door of the house.

8 Moisten the surface. Use a no. 8 deerfoot to stipple foliage on the tree to the left of the house and the bush in front of the porch with a small amount of Lima Green and Dark Forest Green. Stipple the lilac trees in the fields on a premoistened surface using a small amount of Lilac. Lightly stipple in the foliage in front of the house using a double-loaded deerfoot of Dark Forest Green into Lima Green.

9 Using a 6/0 liner paint the small flowers as follows: small one-strokes using Black Cherry tipped into White for the tulips, small one-strokes of Sunbright Yellow for the daffodils and dots of Lavender for the hyacinths, highlighted with dots of Lilac.

SUMMER

10 Using a no. 4 deerfoot double loaded into Dark Forest Green and Celery Green, softly stipple rows of crops curving down the background hill. On a surface premoistened with clean water, stipple in the background hills with Dark Forest Green. Pull faint lines for the tree trunks into the background tree area with a 6/0 liner and thinned Dark Burnt Umber. Highlight the top edge of the front hill with a soft side load float of Celery Green painted on a premoistened surface.

11 The painting procedure for this step is exactly the same as for step 7. Please turn to page 104 for complete instructions.

12 Lightly moisten the surface. Use a no. 8 deerfoot to stipple the foliage onto the trees, bushes and by the path with a double load of Dark Forest Green into Medium Foliage Green.

13 Using a no. 2 flat double loaded into Purple and Bahama Purple plus a touch of White, paint small touches to indicate flower petals. Paint the pink flowers using the same brush and technique, double loaded into Wild Rose and Sachet Pink. Pick up a little White on the Sachet Pink corner of the brush occasionally to add highlight to the flower petals.

AUTUMN

14 Using a no. 4 deerfoot double loaded into Dark Forest Green and Forest Green, softly stipple rows of crops curving down the background hill. On a premoistened surface, stipple in the background hills with Dark Forest Green. Pull faint lines to indicate tree trunks in the background tree area with a 6/0 liner and thinned Dark Burnt Umber. Moisten the surface and highlight the top edge of the front hill with a soft side-load float of Medium Foliage Green.

15 The painting procedure for this step is exactly the same as for step 7. Please turn to page 104 for complete instructions.

16 Lightly moisten the surface and use a no. 8 deerfoot for the foliage. Stipple the orange tree with Tangerine, the yellow tree with Opaque Yellow and the red tree with True Red. Stipple in the bush in front of the porch with a double-loaded no. 8 deerfoot of Opaque Yellow and Medium Foliage Green. Stipple in the foliage next to the path with Medium Foliage Green.

17 Using the tip of a no. 1 liner, scatter dots in the following colors to indicate the autumn flowers in front of the house: Burnt Sienna, Cadmium Orange, Opaque Yellow, Sunbright Yellow. Use a no. 2 flat and Cadmium Orange to paint the small ovals to indicate the pumpkins in the field. Highlight one side of each pumpkin with a side-load float of Pumpkin.

WINTER

18 Moisten the surface with clean water, and use a no. 4 deerfoot to lightly stipple the background trees with Payne's Grey. Side-load float Payne's Grey on a no. 12 flat, and shade to separate between the hills and along the lower edge of the drawer. Paint the snow drifts and highlight the tops of the hills with a strong side-load float of White. Using a no. 8 deerfoot, paint mounds of clouds with White in the sky area.

19 Please see step 7 on page 104 for complete instructions. Add linework of White to some of the tree branches to indicate snow on the trees. Basecoat the snowman with a stipple of White.

20 Use a 6/0 liner and Dark Burnt Umber for the tiny twig arms on the snowman. Dot his eyes and buttons with Black. Paint a line of Cadmium Orange for the carrot nose. Using a no. 12 flat and White, reinforce the snow areas with a strong side-load float. Use the chisel edge of a no. 8 flat double loaded into Dark Forest Green and Medium Foliage Green to stipple in the small pine trees in front of the house. Highlight the edges of some pine tree branches with touches of White.

CUSTOMIZING YOUR RECIPE BOX

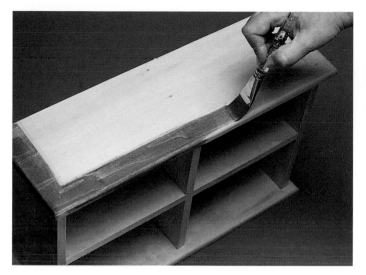

21 Use your transparent tape to create a border by taping off 1¼ inches (3.2cm) in from the front and sides of the top of the recipe box. Wash this band with slightly thinned Dark Forest Green using a 1 inch (25mm) flat. Remove the tape and let the band of color dry completely.

22 Use a no. 1 liner and slightly thinned Burnt Sienna for the stripe on the inside edge of the band. This will cover up any areas where the paint may have leaked under the tape in step 21. Using the same liner and Black, paint the lettering border. Dot the ends of the letters using a stylus and Black.

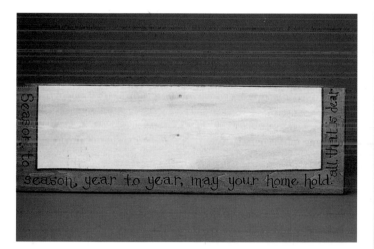

23 Use the saying provided, or customize your recipe box with family names or your favorite message.

24 Erase any visible pattern lines. Varnish to protect your painting with two to three layers of satin acrylic varnish. Brush on the varnish, let cure twenty-four hours and sand lightly between coats.

Celebration Floor Cloth

Floor cloths have become a popular item to paint. They are inexpensive, fun to paint and fun to use in your home. This floor cloth is done with a Fourth of July theme, so meaningful to the United States, but I think it could be easily changed to the colors and flags of any nation. The center of the cloth is filled with a wonderful display of fireworks. Maybe you have a favorite firework display you could include in the center.

paint colors

(D) = Delta Ceramcoat Acrylics; (DA) = DecoArt Americana

White (D)	Raw Linen (D)	Old Parchment (D)	Khaki Tan (DA)	Driftwood (D)	Silver Pine (D)	Stonewedge Green (D)
Light Timberline Green (D)	Jade Green (DA)	Medium Foliage Green (D)	Forest Green (D)	Dark Forest Green (D)	Blue Spruce (D)	Black Green (DA)
Chambray Blue (D)	Tide Pool Blue (D)	Cape Cod Blue (D)	Williamsburg Blue (D)	Liberty Blue (D)	Purple Smoke (D)	Blue Storm (D)
Opaque Blue (D)	Midnight Blue (D)	Cayenne (D)	Opaque Red (D)	Burgundy Rose (D)	Barn Red (D)	Black (D)
Rain Grey (D)	Charcoal Grey (DA)	Charcoal (D)	Spice Brown (D)	Burnt Umber (D)	Dark Burnt Umber (D)	Shimmering Silver (DA)
Pale Gold (D)	14 K Gold (D)	Emperor's Gold (DA)	Copper (DA)	Sparkle Glaze (D)	Sky Blue Pearl (DA)	Ice Blue (D)
Dark Foliage Green (D)						

materials

SURFACE

❧ Pre-primed 2' x 3' (61cm x 91cm) floor cloth is available from your local craft store. Also available through Art Essentials, Alpha, Ohio.

BRUSHES

❧ 1-inch (25mm) flat

❧ 1 inch (25mm) mop

❧ nos. 4 and 8 deerfoot stipple brushes

❧ no. 0 script liner

❧ nos. 2, 4, 12 and 16 flats

ADDITIONAL SUPPLIES

❧ 2-inch (51mm) foam brush or foam paint roller for basecoating the cloth

❧ Delta Sparkle Glaze

❧ acrylic varnish

111

The patterns

This pattern may be hand-traced or photocopied for personal use only. Enlarge at 200%, and then at 125% to return to full size.

BASECOAT CLOTH *and* THE SKY

1 Basecoat the entire cloth with Tide Pool Blue. This may take two coats for a smooth coverage. You can sand lightly between coats. Basecoat the paths to the houses and the road around the complete outer edge in Driftwood. Coat the hills and grass areas in Forest Green using a no. 16 flat. You may go to the directions for each house and basecoat all of the houses, or basecoat one at a time as you go around the floor cloth.

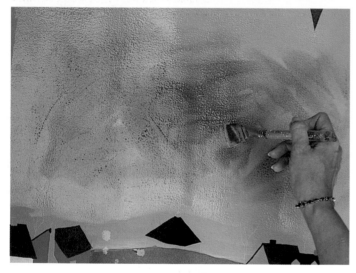

2 Wet the entire sky area with clean water using a 1-inch (25mm) flat. Slip-slap Liberty Blue into the center of the sky area. Quickly add some slip-slaps of Blue Storm and then Purple Smoke.

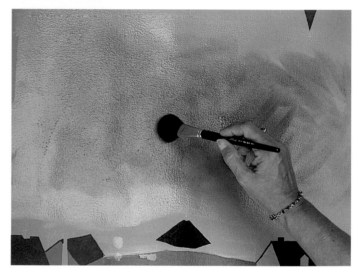

3 Soften these colors into each other with a dry 1-inch (25mm) mop brush. Keep drying your mop on a paper towel as you work the colors into each other. Let the center dry and then repeat steps 2 and 3 until you achieve your desired darkness in the center of the sky area. If the dark center area gets too close to the houses and hills, soften the edges of the dark center with a float of Tide Pool Blue. With the 1-inch (25mm) flat, side-load float Chambray Blue around the tops of the hills.

HILLS *and* PATHS

4 Basecoat the hills with Forest Green. Shade the bottom of the hills and next to the paths with Dark Forest Green. Highlight with any combination of the following colors: Medium Foliage Green, Jade Green, Light Timberline Green and Stonewedge Green. Highlight the crop field behind the large barn with Light Timberline Green. Stipple in the rows of crops in the field with a no. 4 deerfoot using any combination of the greens from your palette. After the crops dry, shade the bottom of the field with a side-load float of Spice Brown using a no. 16 flat.

5 Double load a no. 12 flat with Driftwood and Charcoal Grey. Shade along the edges of the paths and road next to the grass with Charcoal Grey. Keep the streaks on the paths parallel with the edge of the floor cloth. Occasionally streak the paths with touches of Raw Linen. Shade under each door with a side load float of Charcoal Grey. For the two small barns on the back hills, softly streak the paths with a brush mix of Spice Brown and Charcoal Grey using a no. 12 flat.

HINT ❥ *The advantage of having a neutral-colored path around the outside edge of the cloth is if the floor cloth gets damaged, you can trim away the strings and easily repaint the edge with Driftwood.*

THE BLUE HOUSE

6 Basecoat the blue house in Cape Cod Blue. Shade with Charcoal, and highlight with a brush mix of Cape Cod Blue and White using a no. 16 flat. Basecoat the door in Khaki Tan, the floor of the porch in Burnt Umber and the chimney in Barn Red.

7 Using a no. 4 flat, basecoat the windows in with Midnight Blue. Shade the door with Burnt Umber and highlight with Raw Linen. Shade the porch area on the left side and under the roof again with a soft float of Charcoal. Paint the front steps with two strokes of a double loaded no. 2 flat using Charcoal into White. Shade the chimney with a brush mix of Burnt Umber and Barn Red. With a no. 2 flat, lightly stroke on bricks on the chimney with Barn Red and a touch of Raw Linen added. Paint the roof and roof lines using Charcoal highlighted with White. Draw all of the trim lines around the roof, windows and door with White using a no. 0 liner.

8 Softly shade to the right side of the door and each window with a side-load float of Charcoal using a no. 12 flat. Paint all of the porch posts and railings with White using a no. 0 liner. Basecoat the flag in White, the blue field in Opaque Blue with dots of White for the stars and Opaque Red for the red stripes.

9 Paint the tree trunks and branches using Dark Burnt Umber highlighted with touches of Khaki Tan. Start the foliage of the deciduous tree and bushes with Dark Forest Green using a no. 8 deerfoot, then highlight with touches of Medium Foliage Green and Jade Green. Stipple the pine tree on the chisel edge of a no. 12 flat with a double load of Dark Forest Green and Jade Green. Create the flowers around the complete floor cloth with dots of White, Opaque Red and Opaque Blue and/or mixes of the three colors.

THE GAZEBO

10 Basecoat the roof in Black and highlight with White. Paint the floor in Charcoal Grey streaked with Raw Linen for the wood grain. Keep the streaks parallel with the edge of the floor cloth. Paint the back posts and railings first with White and add a touch of Charcoal Grey.

11 Use White and a no. 0 liner for the linework on the front posts, railings, trim under the roof and curved supports at the tops of the posts. Using a no. 2 flat double loaded with Black and White, stroke on the front steps. Each step going down is wider than the step above it. Basecoat the ball finials and flagpole with Emperor's Gold, shaded with Copper and highlight with Pale Gold using a no. 2 flat and no. 0 liner.

12 Basecoat the flag, bunting and rosettes in White, Opaque Red and Opaque Blue. After the flag is painted and dry, add a flip-flop float of Charcoal Grey to create a soft wave in it. Paint the flag rope with Black. Use a no. 0 liner and pull thin stripes of the red, blue and then white for the bunting. Create the rosettes by painting a center dot of Opaque Red, surrounded by a circle of White and then a circle of Opaque Blue.

13 Stipple in the flower foliage using a no. 8 deerfoot with Dark Foliage Green, Medium Foliage Green and Jade Green. Stipple in the pine trees using the chisel edge of a no. 12 flat with a double load of Dark Forest Green and Jade Green. Paint the geranium blossoms with dots of Opaque Red and surround them by dot flowers of Opaque Blue, White or any combination of these colors.

CREAM *and* BLUE HOUSES

14 Basecoat the cream house with Old Parchment, shade with Burnt Umber plus a touch of Charcoal Grey and highlight with Raw Linen using a no. 16 flat. Paint the door of the cream house with Williamsburg Blue. Basecoat the blue house in Williamsburg Blue, shade with Charcoal and highlight with a mix of Williamsburg Blue plus a touch of White. Basecoat the chimneys in Barn Red, and the door of the blue house in Khaki Tan.

15 Shade the Khaki Tan door on the left side with Burnt Umber, and highlight on the right with Raw Linen. Shade the blue door with Charcoal, and highlight with a mix of Williamsburg Blue plus a touch of White. Base the windows on both houses with Midnight Blue using a no. 4 flat. Shade the chimneys with Burnt Umber. Stroke in the bricks with Barn Red plus a touch of Raw Linen using a no. 2 flat. Side-load float White on a no. 4 flat to create curtain valences. Use a light touch and ruffle the bottom edge of the valences. Use a no. 0 liner and White for all the linework of the trim and outlines. Create the door steps with a double-loaded stroke of Charcoal and White using a no. 2 flat. Stroke in the window boxes on the cream house with a double load of Williamsburg Blue and Charcoal using a no. 2 flat. Keep the dark color to the bottom of the window box.

16 Start the bunting on the house with a stripe of Opaque Red, next a stripe of White, followed with a stripe of Opaque Blue. Tie them to the roof of the house with a stroke of Opaque Blue and a touch of White. Paint the flagpole in Black with a knob of Emperor's Gold on the top. Use a no. 0 liner for the bunting and the flagpole. Paint the flag with White, Opaque Blue and Opaque Red using a no. 2 flat for the basecoat and a no. 0 liner for the stripes. Paint the tree trunk using Dark Burnt Umber with touches of Raw Linen using a no. 0 liner. Using a ¾-inch (19mm) flat and a soft side-load float of Dark Burnt Umber, shade between the two houses on the blue house and on the addition to the cream house.

17 Start the foliage in the window boxes, around the base of the houses and the tree with a light stipple of Dark Forest Green using a no. 8 deerfoot. Highlight the foliage with a light stipple of Medium Foliage Green and/or Jade Green. Stipple in the pine tree with a double load of Dark Forest Green and Jade Green using the chisel edge of a no. 12 flat. Dot in the flowers in the window boxes with Opaque Red and White, and Opaque Blue and White. Paint the flowers in the bushes with White. Add a soft flip-flop float of Charcoal Grey on the flag to make it fold.

THE CHURCH

Paint the roof Charcoal and shade the steeple sections with Black. Highlight with White.

The cross and doorknobs are Emperor's Gold. The cross is shaded with Copper.

Outline the windows, doors and steeple with White and a no. o liner.

Use a no. 2 flat and a brush mix of Raw Linen, Spice Brown and Charcoal Grey for the bricks.

Base the building with Raw Linen, shade with Spice Brown and a touch of Charcoal Grey and highlight with White.

Complete the foliage with same colors and techniques as previously described.

Crosshatch the windows with fine lines of White.

Base the windows with thinned Midnight Blue using a no. 8 flat.

Create the steps with a no. 2 flat double-loaded with Black and White.

Base the door in Spice Brown and shade with Charcoal Grey.

This pattern may be hand-traced or photocopied for personal use only. Enlarge at 167% to return to full size.

THE GREEN HOUSE

The flag rope is a brush mix of Black and White.

Paint the flag pole with Black with a ball of Emperor's Gold.

Base the flag with White, with a field of Opaque Blue with White dots. Stripes are Opaque Red.

Outline the windows, doors and roof line with Raw Linen and a no. 0 liner.

The roof is based with Charcoal and highlighted with White.

Use a no. 16 flat and Silver Pine for the house. Shade with a brush mix of Black Green and Charcoal Grey. Highlight with a brush mix of Silver Pine and Raw Linen.

The chimney is a brush mix of Barn Red and Spice Brown. Shade with Charcoal Grey and a no. 4 flat.

The bricks on the chimney are a brush mix of Barn Red and Charcoal Grey with a no. 4 flat.

The foliage is completed using colors and techniques previously described.

The bricks on the house are brush mix of Blue Spruce plus a touch of Raw Linen and Charcoal with no. 2 flat.

The rosettes are a center dot of Opaque Red, encircled by ring of White and surrounded by Opaque Blue. Use the three colors for the streamers.

Paint the fence with Raw Linen using a no. 0 liner. Shade posts with a soft stroke of Charcoal Grey pulling up from the bottom. Highlight post with White from the top.

Use a no. 8 flat and Raw Linen for the door. Shade with Charcoal Grey.

Base in the windows with thinned Midnight Blue using a no. 8 flat.

Use Blue Spruce with a no. 2 flat for the shutters.

The patterns on pages 120 and 121 may be hand-traced or photocopied for personal use only. Enlarge the pattern on page 120 at 167% to return to full size.

RED BARNS

All windows are Midnight Blue.

All roofs are Black highlighted with White.

Detail the silo ladder with fine lines of Black using a no. o liner.

The silo is based with Rain Grey, shaded with Charcoal and highlighted with White.

The flag is based with Raw Linen, with a field of Opaque Blue and a touch of Charcoal added. Stripes are Barn Red and the single star is White.

Paint the fence with Raw Linen and shade with Charcoal Grey from the bottom. Do not highlight.

The stone foundation is Charcoal Grey. Dab in stones with a no. 1 round and a brush mix of Charcoal, White and Charcoal Grey.

Basecoat all barns with Barn Red, shade with Charcoal Grey and highlight with Opaque Red. Highlight again as needed with Opaque Red, lightened with a touch of Raw Linen.

Enlarge the pattern at 133% to return to full size.

RED BARNS, *continued*

The foliage is completed using the colors and techniques previously described.

Outline all windows, door trims and under the roofs with White and a no. o liner.

Base the silo with Rain Grey, shade with Charcoal and highlight with White.

The door frames are floats of Charcoal Grey.

Basecoat all barns with Barn Red, shade with Charcoal Grey and highlight with Opaque Red. Highlight again as needed with Opaque Red, lightened with a touch of Raw Linen.

All roofs are Black highlighted with White.

The patterns on pages 122 and 123 may be photocopied or hand-traced for personal use only. The top barn is shown at full size. Enlarge the bottom barn 111% to return to full size.

IVORY, TAN *and* BRICK HOUSES

The siding lines are Burnt Umber.

All windows are Midnight Blue with a no. 4 flat.

Paint the roof Charcoal highlighted with White.

Outline all windows, doors and roof lines with White and no. 0 liner.

All chimneys are Barn Red and highlighted with a brush mix Barn Red and Raw Linen.

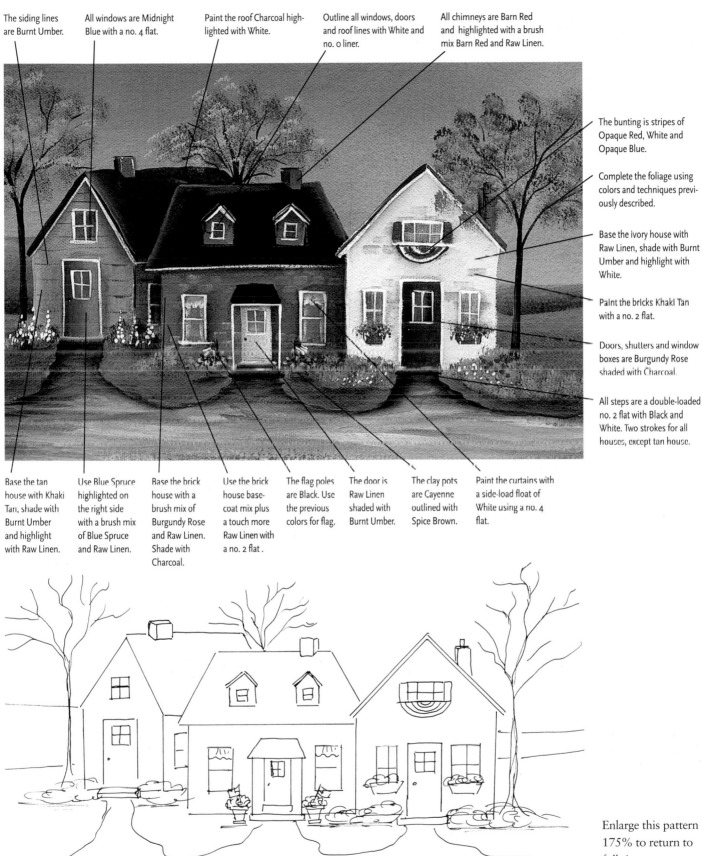

The bunting is stripes of Opaque Red, White and Opaque Blue.

Complete the foliage using colors and techniques previously described.

Base the ivory house with Raw Linen, shade with Burnt Umber and highlight with White.

Paint the bricks Khaki Tan with a no. 2 flat.

Doors, shutters and window boxes are Burgundy Rose shaded with Charcoal.

All steps are a double-loaded no. 2 flat with Black and White. Two strokes for all houses, except tan house.

Base the tan house with Khaki Tan, shade with Burnt Umber and highlight with Raw Linen.

Use Blue Spruce highlighted on the right side with a brush mix of Blue Spruce and Raw Linen.

Base the brick house with a brush mix of Burgundy Rose and Raw Linen. Shade with Charcoal.

Use the brick house base-coat mix plus a touch more Raw Linen with a no. 2 flat .

The flag poles are Black. Use the previous colors for flag.

The door is Raw Linen shaded with Burnt Umber.

The clay pots are Cayenne outlined with Spice Brown.

Paint the curtains with a side-load float of White using a no. 4 flat.

Enlarge this pattern 175% to return to full size.

123

FIREWORKS

22 Adding sparkling fireworks to the center sky area turns your floor cloth into a celebration!

1. Paint long, thin lines and stars on the ends of the lines with 14 K Gold. Dot the centers of these stars with Shimmering Silver. Paint dots around the center and extra dots around the outside stars in Emperor's Gold.

2. Begin with dots in the shape of a star with Shimmering Silver. Create the burst lines from the end of each point and in the center with 14 K Gold. Surround them by more dots of Shimmering Silver.

3. Load a no. 1 liner with Copper and tip the brush into Pale Gold. Pull comma strokes in toward the center dot of Pale Gold. Surround the center with dots of Copper and Pale Gold. The Pale Gold tips of the strokes should be at the outside of the fireworks to indicate the brightest light that fades toward the center.

4. Begin with dots of Opaque Red mixed with Sparkle Glaze in curved lines coming from the center. Paint the burst lines at the center and at the end of each red line of dots using a brush mix of Ice Blue and Sky Blue Pearl. Surround the burst lines with dots of Shimmering Silver.

5. Paint all lines, curlicues and burst lines with 14 K Gold. Highlight the tops of some straight lines and the upper curves of the curlicues with Shimmering Silver. The dots in the center of the burst lines are Shimmering Silver.

6. Paint all of the lines and burst lines using Emperor's Gold with dots of Copper.

These patterns may be hand-traced or photocopied for personal use only. To return the pattern to full size you must first enlarge the pattern 200%, then enlarge that pattern 200%.

SET-BACK SHADING *and* VARNISH

23 Set back one building or part of a building behind another building with a set-back float using a ¾-inch (19mm) flat. Side-load float Dark Burnt Umber plus a touch of Charcoal Grey. Float this on the back buildings right next to the front building with the darkest color right next to the front building. This helps give some depth to the painting. Allow the painting to dry thoroughly, erase any visible tracing lines and varnish with at least three coats of your favorite acrylic varnish. Also, apply one coat of varnish to the back side of the floor cloth.

Resources

ART ESSENTIALS, INC.
670 Orchard Lane
Rt. 35, Box 148
Alpha, OH 45301
Phone (937) 426-3503
Fax: (937) 426-9726

DECOART
P.O. Box 327
Stanford, KY 40484
Phone: (606) 365-3193
Fax: (606) 365-9739
E-mail: paint@decoart.com
Web site: www.decoart.com

DELTA TECHNICAL COATINGS, INC.
2550 Pellissier Place
Whittier, CA 90601
Phone: (800) 423-4135
Fax: (562) 695-5157
Web site: www.deltacrafts.com

DESIGNS BY BENTWOOD, INC.
P.O. Box 1676
Thomasville, GA 31799-1676
Phone: (912) 226-1223
Fax: (912) 228-5251

J.W. ETC.
2205 First St., Suite 103
Simi Valley, CA 93065
Phone: (805) 526-5066
Fax: (805) 526-1297
E-mail: jwetc@earthlink.net
Web site: www.jwetc.com

PESKY BEAR
5059 Roszyk Hill Rd.
Machias, NY 14101
Phone/ Fax: (716) 942-3250

SCHARFF BRUSHES, INC.
P.O. Box 746
Fayetteville, GA 30214
Phone: (888) SCHARFF or (770) 461-2200
Fax: (770) 461-2472
E-mail: scharff@artbrush.com
Web site: www.artbrush.com

VIKING WOODCRAFTS, INC.
1317 8th Street SE
Waseca, MN 56093
Phone: (507) 835-8043
Fax: (507) 835-3895
E-mail: viking@platec.net
Web site: www.vikingwoodcrafts.com

WAYNE'S WOODENWARE
Wayne and Joan Stabnaw
102C Fieldcrest Drive
Neenah, WI 54956
Phone: (920) 725-7986
Fax: (920) 725-9386
For orders only: (800) 840-1497

WOODCRAFTS
Art and Betty Hall
P.O. Box 78
Hwy. 67W
Bicknell, IN 47512-0078
Phone: (812) 735-4829
Fax: (812) 735-3187
For orders only: (800) 733-4820

The following Canadian retailers may also carry the supplies used in this book:

CRAFTS CANADA
2745 29th St. NE
Calgary, ON
T1Y 7B5

FOLK ART ENTERPRISES
P.O. Box 1088
Ridgetown, ON
NOP 2CO
Phone: (888) 214-0062

MacPHERSON CRAFT WHOLESALE
83 Queen St. E.
PO Box 1870
St. Mary's, ON
N4X 1C2
Phone: (519) 284-1741

MAUREEN McNAUGHTON ENTERPRISES
RR #2
Bellwood, ON
NOB 1JO
Phone: (519) 843-5648

MERCURY ART & CRAFT SUPERSHOP
332 Wellington St.
London, ON
N6C 4P7
Phone: (519) 434-1636

TOWN & COUNTRY FOLK ART SUPPLIES
93 Green Lane
Thornhill, ON
L3T 6K6
Phone: (905) 882-0199

Index

Explore Decorative Painting with North Light Books!

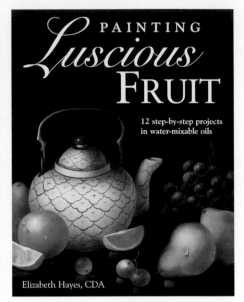

Learn to paint your favorite Christmas themes, including Santas, angels, elves and more, on everything from glittering ornaments to festive albums with these nine all-new, step-by-step projects from renowned decorative painter, John Gutcher.

He makes mastering those tricky details simple with special tips for painting fur, hair, richly-textured clothing and realistic flesh tones. Just follow along with John to create a range of wonderful holiday heirlooms!

1-58180-105-X, paperback, 128 pages

Fantastic treasures await you, hidden among piles of junk at garage sales and swap meets. With this book, you'll be able to transform these spectacular bargains into the kind of art and furniture you'd be proud to have in your home, plus you'll have a great time in the process!

In ten gorgeous step-by-step projects, author and artist Kerry Trout shows you how to choose flea market finds and turn them into fabulous family heirlooms.

1-58180-092-4, paperback, 144 pages

Let Elizabeth Hayes, CDA help you harvest a bounty of fresh-picked fruit in your paintings, from blueberries and cherries to apples, bananas and melons. Her detailed, friendly instruction and twelve easy step-by-step projects will show you how to paint fruit that looks good enough to eat.

Whether you're an absolute beginner or an experienced painter, you'll learn how to fill your home with luscious, ripe fruit. The hardest thing will be selecting which project you'll start first.

1-58180-078-9, paperback, 128 pages

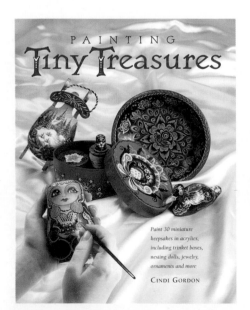

Learn to paint miniature decorative painting masterpieces with these 14 full-color, step-by-step projects, including Victorian vanity boxes, wooden nesting dolls, holiday ornaments and more.

All the instructions are supplemented with hints and sidebars, complete materials lists, color palettes and designs ready to be hand traced or photocopied. A glossary of terms and techniques completes the package so that you'll never be without guidance.

0-89134-992-8, paperback, 128 pages

Mount Laurel Library
100 Walt Whitman Avenue
Mt. Laurel, NJ 08054-9539
(856) 234-7319